Bond

How to do …
11+ English

Liz Heesom

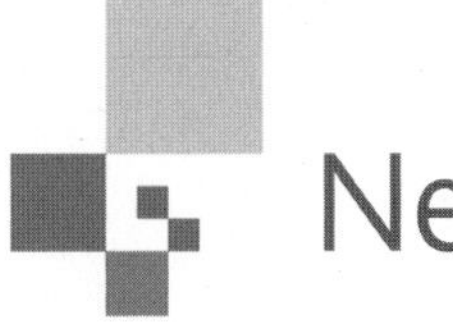

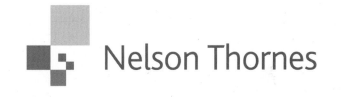

Nelson Thornes

Published in 2006 by:
Nelson Thornes Ltd
Delta Place
27 Bath Road
CHELTENHAM
GL53 7TH
United Kingdom

10 11 12 / 10 9 8 7

A catalogue record for this book is available from the British Library

ISBN: 978 0 7487 9695 3

Cover photograph: Jigsaw by Bananastock/Cadmium RF (NT)
Page make-up by GreenGate Publishing Services

Printed and bound in Croatia by Zrinski

Acknowledgements

Extract from *Ant's Pants* reproduced by permission of The Agency (London) Ltd © Steve Skidmore and Steve Barlow 1990. First published by Oxford University Press 1990. All rights reserved and enquiries to The Agency (London) Ltd, 24 Pottery Lane, London W11 4LZ. Fax 0207 727 9037.

"Painted Pots" by Ray Gibson reproduced from *The Usborne Book of Making Presents* by permission of Usborne Publishing, 83–85 Saffron Hill, London, EC1N 8RT, UK. www.usborne.com Copyright © Usborne Publishing Ltd.

Extract from *How Science Works* by Judith Hann reproduced with the permission of the Reader's Digest Association, UK.

Extract from *Cider with Rosie* by Laurie Lee, published by Hogarth Press. Reprinted by permission of The Random House Group Ltd.

Extract from *The Ghost of Thomas Kempe* by Penelope Lively copyright © 1973 reproduced with permission from Egmont UK.

Extract from *Eyewitness: Sharks* by Miranda MacQuitty (Dorling Kindersley, 1998). Text copyright © Miranda MacQuitty, 1998. Copyright © Dorling Kindersley, 1998.

"The Fawn" by Edna St Vincent Millay. All rights reserved. Copyright © 1934, 1962 by Edna St Vincent Millay and Norma Millay Ellis. Reprinted by permission of Elizabeth Barnett, Literary Executor, The Millay Society.

Extract from *Why the Whales Came* by Michael Morpurgo reproduced by permission of David Higham Associates.

Extract from *Cannery Row* by John Steinbeck (Penguin Books, 2000) copyright © 1945 by John Steinbeck.

Extract from 'A Prospect of the Sea' in *Collected Stories* by Dylan Thomas reproduced by permission of David Higham Associates.

Contents

Introduction

"I hate literacy."

"Reading is boring."

"I find doing comprehension difficult."

"When I have to write a story, I can't think what to write."

"Why is English so hard to spell?"

Children have to use and respond to English in many different ways during primary school. Being put to the test for the 11+ exam can be rather daunting if they are anxious or unsure about what they have to do.

The 11+/selective examinations system is still used to decide grammar and independent school entry in several parts of the UK. Depending on the requirements set by each Local Education Authority (LEA) and/or individual schools, children sitting the 11+ exam will complete one or more papers in the following subjects: maths, English, non-verbal reasoning and verbal reasoning. Your child's primary school should automatically inform you about these entrance exams once your child is in Year 5 but you can contact your LEA for more details before this.

The contents of this book are relevant to all children who are preparing for the English paper for 11+/selective exams which they will take during their final year (Year 6) at primary school. *How to do 11+ English* can also be used as a key resource to support more general practice in English.

1 What is an 11+ English exam?

An 11+ English exam may differ from region to region, but a paper will generally consist of:

- **Comprehension** exercises, where children have to read pieces of text and answer questions on them.
- **Writing** tasks, where children have to write something themselves.
- **Grammar** and **punctuation** problems, where children show their understanding of how English works as a language.
- **Spelling** tasks, where children spot incorrect spellings.

There are two different formats for 11+ English exam papers. Questions can either be presented in a **standard** or a **multiple-choice** layout. Standard is where a child writes his or her answers on the question paper. Multiple-choice is where possible answers are given on the paper and a child marks his or her chosen answer in a separate booklet.

The practice exercises in *How to do 11+ English* are mostly written in a standard format, although some multiple-choice tasks are included.

As with all exams, 11+ English papers are timed and they usually last from 45 minutes to one hour. Children therefore need to complete timed tests as well as working through non-timed practice, so they can see what they are able to do within a given time frame.

2 How can you use this book?

How to do 11+ English is a practical guide designed for use by children, but it also has a wealth of essential advice and tips for adults involved in 11+ practice. The book works through the components that make up 11+ English papers, teaching and practising the skills needed to succeed in these exams. It tells children (and parents!) what to expect and provides sound strategies that can be practised and developed further.

It may not be necessary to work through all of the sections provided in this book because your child may already be quite confident in several areas. However, if there are areas where your child feels hesitant, needs to reinforce what he or she knows or learn new techniques, then these sections should be worked through in detail, as this will help to build confidence and clear up any confusion. By using the central pull-out test as a guide, you will be able to see in which parts of 11+ English your child may need further practice.

How to do 11+ English is part of the well-known and long-established Bond series, whose finely-graded 11+ resources have been trusted by parents, teachers and tutors for over 40 years. This book accompanies the range of *Bond Assessment Papers in English*, which provide a variety of additional practice for 11+ English skills. The book can also be used to complement other general English textbooks.

3 How is this book organised?

This book is divided into sections which cover the skills most commonly tested in 11+ English papers. (You should contact your LEA or your child's primary school to confirm the format of the paper in your area, as not all 11+ English exams follow the same model. For instance, a creative writing task is not always included.)

At school all children should learn the skills and content covered in this book and will be tested on all these elements at some stage, so each section is useful for general reference, practice and confidence-building.

There are six main sections to this book:

A Where do you start?
B Comprehension
C Writing
D Grammar and punctuation
E Spelling
F How do you prepare for the exam?

Section A provides clear guidance on the key knowledge and skills every child needs to have before starting more focused practice for 11+ English. It is important that you and your child find out which key skills you may need to practise together. The tips in this section give essential advice on how to check and improve your child's basic skills.

Sections B–E show the common tasks that children may have to do in 11+ English exams. Each of these tasks is described with:

- explanations
- practice activities – to be completed in this book 

  – to be completed in a notebook 
- advice for children and parents' hints

Section F provides essential advice on exam technique and on preparing for the exam day itself.

The **central pull-out section** contains an 11+ English practice paper. If you wish to set this as a 'before and after' test please visit www.bond11plus.co.uk and follow the Free Resources link to download another free copy. The answers to all the exercises are at the end of the main **Answers** section.

There is also a **glossary** towards the end of the book, which contains brief explanations of words or terms used in 11+ English.

To accompany this book, some free electronic materials are also available for you to download from our web site at www.bond11plus.co.uk. Where online materials relate to sections of this book, the following icon appears in the margin. www

4 *When should you start practising?*

A good time to check up on basic skills is the summer term of Year 4. That gives you the summer holidays to:

Checklist

- ✓ practise and reinforce any knowledge or skills that are a little shaky
- ✓ stock up on reading materials
- ✓ keep a diary or write a summer project.

Once your child is settled into Year 5, it is important to establish a regular routine of bedtime reading (if that's not already part of your child's life) and a couple of quiet, uninterrupted sessions a week for practice.

This would also be a good time to try the central pull-out test to see how your child copes with 11+ English tasks, as well as the English placement tests provided in *The Parents' Guide to the 11+*. (See the inside cover for details.)

5 What do you need?

Checklist

- ✓ A stock of **pencils**, a good quality **pencil sharpener** and a supply of **erasers**.
- ✓ A **library card** and access to a library.
- ✓ Wide-spaced, good quality lined **exercise books**, preferably stapled. It is a good idea to keep your child's work in these, as bits of paper get scrappy or lost and it is lovely to look back to see the progress!
- ✓ A small **kitchen timer** that can be used by your child for timed or speed work.
- ✓ A good **dictionary** and **thesaurus** (not children's versions by this stage).
- ✓ Access to **drinking water**.
- ✓ A **quiet**, **well-lit space** to work in.

A Where do you start?

1 Check basic skills

It is important to find out whether your child is capable of tackling 11+ English. Your child will need above all to be able to read fluently, accurately and with understanding. These key skills underpin all other skills in all aspects of 11+ testing.

Your child will also need to be able to **write clearly and coherently** and be able to **understand terms** used in English work such as **punctuation**, **alphabetical order**, **parts of speech** (noun, verb, adjective, adverb, connective, pronoun), **spelling terms** (syllable, vowel, consonant, prefix, suffix) and **instructions**.

Talk with your child's teacher and find out what he or she thinks. You may be able to find out your child's predicted mark for the Year 6 National Curriculum Test. (These are often still referred to as the SATs – Standard Assessment Tests.) At the end of Year 6, children aged about 11 are expected to achieve level 4 in English, maths and science.

If your child is already aged 10 or 11, you could try giving him or her the pull-out test from the middle of this book to see how he or she performs on an 11+ style paper. This can be used as a 'before and after' 11+ practice test if you download a second free copy from our website and time your child on both occasions. (The English placement test found in *The Parents' Guide to the 11+* is also a useful gauge of your child's ability level. See the inside cover for details.)

Whatever stage your child is at, you may find it useful to find out what he or she knows already and this will help to point towards things to practise before moving on to more focused 11+ practice. Here are some things to try out with your child:

- Say and spell the days of the week.
- Say and spell the months.
- Write his or her name and address.
- Spell number words up to 20 and the 10s numbers up to 100.
- Say the alphabet quickly and spot the vowels.
- Clap and count the syllables in words like 'disappointment' or 'unbelievable'.
- Ask what the opposite of (hot, quiet, delicious…) is.
- Read something from a newspaper and talk about it together.
- Retell a familiar story.

PARENT TIP

Try out these things casually, at a time when your child is relaxed and keen to show what he or she knows. Weekends or holidays, when nothing else is going on, may be good moments.

② *Help your child to read*

The ability to read fluently, widely, happily and meaningfully is the fundamental key to 11+ English success.

The basis for reading lies in earliest childhood. Familiarity with books, sharing stories, being read to, talking about words, listening to story tapes, enjoying rhymes and poems, and retelling stories are all a vital part of children's first learning experiences.

By the end of Year 4, aged about eight or nine, children should be showing this familiarity with the written word and be able to read fluently. But it doesn't stop there!

Encourage a love of reading:

- Join a library. Buy, borrow and swap books.
- Get into the reading habit – maybe just before bedtime?
- Buy a bedside light for bedtime reading.
- Talk about books.
- Read to your children as well as hearing them read; you can read something much more demanding than they can yet manage on their own.
- Find favourite authors.
- Try something new, e.g. see children's review pages in newspapers; join a children's book club.
- Listen to story tapes together in the car or alone at bedtime.
- Enjoy poems and non-fiction.
- Subscribe to magazines; share newspaper stories.
- Aim to ration the television and computer!

Encourage vocabulary development:

- Talk about words.
- Play with words: jokes, puns, crosswords, wordsearches.
- Play word games: Scrabble, Boggle, hangman, 20 questions, Yes/No, charades.
- Collect words: make 'juicy words' pages or posters where your child can collect unusual, melodious or exciting words to learn and enjoy.
- Think about meanings using a dictionary or a thesaurus.
- Find extraordinary words to try on friends and family.

Encourage reading improvement:

- Decipher unfamiliar words together, breaking them up into syllables.
- Spot rhyming words.
- Collect 'headline words' from the headlines of broadsheet newspapers, cut them out, practise reading them and discuss meanings and uses.
- Make lists of words your child finds hard to read or pronounce, and practise them together.

What should I do if my child doesn't enjoy reading?

There are children who can read but don't like reading and are reluctant to work at their literacy. Their parents get very anxious about this. What can you do?

Checklist

- ✓ Don't always expect your child to do the reading; reading to your child can be a very enjoyable shared activity.
- ✓ Try different authors and if one gels, help your child to get hold of books by that one.
- ✓ Help motivation: start a book off by reading a few chapters to your child.
- ✓ Sometimes reluctant readers are put off by 'hard' books which their parents or teachers think would be 'good for them' to read. Scooting through easier books with larger print and more pictures can be quite liberating and is still good practice.
- ✓ Try choosing a brand new book together as encouragement.
- ✓ Don't worry if your child prefers non-fiction to fiction, or vice versa; the important thing is to be able to read.
- ✓ Friends are sometimes better 'prodders' than parents or teachers.

Encourage reading techniques such as:

- scanning (finding a piece of information quickly)
- skimming (getting the gist)
- pointing out the key words
- reading the blurb
- reading the introduction
- following instructions
- using the 'three-letter trick': sound out the first three letters and that can give a big hint
- deciphering new words by breaking them up into syllables
- spotting smaller words hidden in longer ones

Reading suggestions

Basic level

If your child isn't yet reading for pleasure, these are suggestions for getting him or her going:

- Humphrey Carpenter: *Mr Majeika* series
- Shorter books by Roald Dahl: *The Magic Finger*; *The Twits*; *Esio Trot*, etc.
- Anne Fine: *Bill's New Frock*; *A Sudden Puff of Glittering Smoke* and sequels
- Dick King-Smith: *The Hodgeheg*; *Clever Duck*; *Friends and Brothers*, etc.
- Lemony Snicket: *A Series of Unfortunate Events*
- Jeremy Strong: *There's a Viking in my Bed*; *Pirate Pandemonium*, etc.
- Jacqueline Wilson: *Cliffhanger*; *The Cat Mummy*; *Buried Alive!*, etc.
- Any Corgi Yearling, Mammoth Read or Young Puffins

Boys

Try books by:

- Eoin Colfer: *Artemis Fowl* series
- Sir Arthur Conan Doyle
- Anthony Horowitz
- Eric Kästner
- Robert Westall

Animal lovers

Try books by:

- Richard Adams
- Colin Dann
- Gerald Durrell: *My Family and Other Animals*
- Brian Jacques: *Redwall* series
- Dick King-Smith
- Anna Sewell: *Black Beauty*
- E.B. White: *Charlotte's Web*

Fantasy and sci-fi lovers

Try books by:

- Peter Dickinson
- Alan Garner
- Brian Jacques
- Robin Jarvis
- Ursula K. Le Guin
- William Nicholson
- Garth Nix
- Lynn Reid Banks
- Jules Verne
- J.R.R. Tolkien
- H.G. Wells
- John Wyndham: *The Day of the Triffids*; *The Kraken Wakes*
- Dianna Wynne Jones

Girls

Try books by:

- Louisa M. Alcott
- Georgia Byng
- Cornelia Funke
- Eva Ibbotson
- Laura Ingalls Wilder
- Jacqueline Wilson

Humour lovers

Try books by:

- Philip Ardagh
- Michael Bond: *Paddington* series
- Helen Cresswell: *Bagthorpes* series
- Richmal Crompton: *William* series
- Roald Dahl
- Terry Jones
- Astrid Lindgren: *Pippi Longstocking* series
- Terry Pratchett

History lovers

Try books by:

- Kevin Crossley-Holland: *Arthur* trilogy
- Terry Deary
- Laura Ingalls Wilder
- Judith Kerr
- Michael Morpurgo
- Rosemary Sutcliff
- Geoffrey Trease
- Henry Treece

Authors to look out for:

- David Almond
- Helen Cresswell
- Gillian Cross
- Michelle Magorian

Short story collections:

There are good collections published by Collins, Kingfisher and Puffin.

Poems:

There are many good children's anthologies. To get children going, try collections by Roger McGough or Benjamin Zephaniah.

Catch up on the classics

- Nina Bawden: *Carrie's War* etc.
- Lewis Carroll: *Alice in Wonderland* etc.
- Daniel Defoe: *Robinson Crusoe*
- Elizabeth Goudge: *The Little White Horse*
- Frances Hodgson Burnett: *The Secret Garden etc.*
- Ted Hughes: *The Iron Man*
- Clive King: *Stig of the Dump*
- Rudyard Kipling: *The Jungle Book*
- C.S. Lewis: *Narnia* series
- Penelope Lively: *The Whispering Knights* etc.
- John Masefield: *The Box of Delights* etc.
- Mary Norton: *The Borrowers* series
- Philippa Pearce: *Tom's Midnight Garden* etc.
- Arthur Ransome: *Swallows and Amazons*
- Robert Louis Stevenson: *Treasure Island*; *Kidnapped*
- Alison Uttley: *A Traveller in Time*

Time for a challenge!

- Jane Austen: *Pride and Prejudice* etc.
- The Brontë sisters: *Wuthering Heights*; *Jane Eyre*
- Charles Dickens: *David Copperfield* etc.
- Alexandre Dumas: *The Black Tulip* etc.
- Jostein Gaarder: *Sophie's World*
- Philip Pullman: *His Dark Materials* trilogy
- J.K. Rowling: *Harry Potter* series
- J.R.R. Tolkien: *The Lord of the Rings*
- Leo Tolstoy: *Anna Karenina*; *War and Peace*

(3) *Help your child to write*

Use every opportunity to encourage your child to write. Here are some suggestions for providing valuable writing practice:

- Keep a diary during the holidays.
- Write shopping lists.
- Write thank-you letters or cards to friends and relatives.
- Write stories to go with a picture.
- Fill in special days on a calendar.
- Take telephone messages by writing them down.

A supply of felt-tip pens, crayons, ink pens and paper or notebooks may encourage independent writing. Having an abandoned old desk diary sometimes encourages children to write. Pen and pencil games using words are also good fun. Try hangman or crosswords. There are many puzzle books available from booksellers or newsagents which can be fun for children to fill in.

But remember: children may not necessarily enjoy writing even if they love books and reading. It can be quite hard work to write when you have only just learnt how to, and children already spend a large part of their school day writing. It's much more difficult to curl up to do a piece of writing than it is to enjoy a book!

B Comprehension

"I find comprehension difficult."

So do many people. You are not alone!

"What does comprehension mean?"

The word means **understanding**.

A comprehension exercise or test can consist of: a passage or passages of text; part of a story; a poem; a piece of information or explanation; a description.

Your job is to read the text and then show that you understand it by answering questions about it. Sometimes the text and the questions can be quite challenging. It can be difficult to understand anything at first.

You need to be:

Checklist

- ✓ a good reader
- ✓ a good thinker
- ✓ a good word-spotter
- ✓ a good detective!

(1) *Recognise question types*

PARENT TIP

You can help here by finding out details of the 11+ exam in your area. (See Introduction.)

11+ English comprehension tests may have different kinds of questions. It depends on the school setting the test or the part of the country you live in.

Multiple-choice questions

This is where several possible answers to a question are given and you have to find the best one.

- Sometimes you underline the correct answer, put a mark in a box or mark a separate answer booklet.
- The answers can all look very similar so you have to find the right part of the text by **scanning** (looking quickly through the text until you come to the part you need) and then do your detective work.
- Never leave out an answer in a multiple-choice test. After all, the answers are all there and you have a good chance of choosing the right one if you make a sensible guess.

Standard questions

Here, the answers are not provided. You have to search the text carefully to answer the questions.

- Often you are asked to write the answers in complete sentences.
- Scan the text to find the right part for each question.
- Be careful to provide all the details the question asks for and write each answer in your own words. Usually, you will find all the information you need in the text.
- Look at the marks given for each question. These are often put in brackets at the end of the question. They can give you a clue about how much to write.

② *Learn how to do comprehension*

"How am I expected to remember a whole passage?"

You're not!

Comprehension is not a memory test. Even if the questions are on a different page or a different sheet, you must always use the text to help you find the answer, even if you think you can remember it.

"How do I begin?"

A useful strategy is to learn this **five-point plan** for doing comprehension.

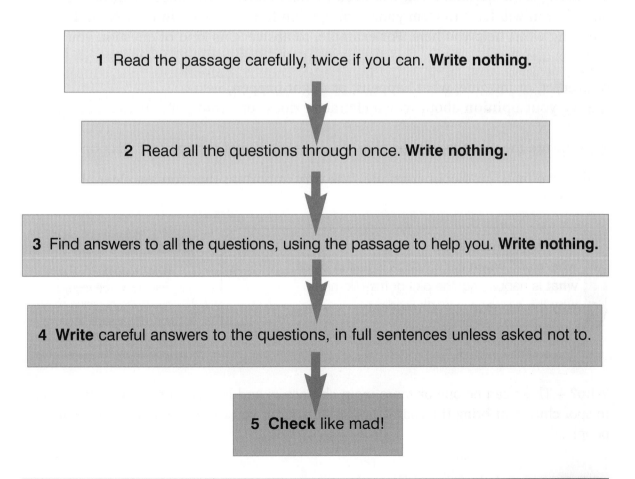

1 Read the passage carefully, twice if you can. **Write nothing.**

2 Read all the questions through once. **Write nothing.**

3 Find answers to all the questions, using the passage to help you. **Write nothing.**

4 **Write** careful answers to the questions, in full sentences unless asked not to.

5 **Check** like mad!

Of course, you may be taught other strategies or develop your own, but this five-point plan is a good way to start. It encourages you to read and think carefully before you start writing answers. This is especially important if the passage is long or difficult to understand.

Never just copy out chunks of text! You will lose marks. Try to use your own words.

"But there are words I don't know."

Yes, there may well be!

Sometimes you may have to explain meanings of words. These words are part of a longer piece of writing, so the text around an unfamiliar word may give you clues. Perhaps the word itself contains clues. It may contain a root word that you recognise or a prefix or a suffix that has a meaning. (See Section E.)

"I don't have any idea what one part of the passage means."

Always have a go, even if you are not sure. Read that paragraph several times, spot the key words and ideas and try to imagine what is going on. It's better to guess and put something, rather than leave a blank.

"I can't find the answer to the question anywhere."

To answer some questions you will need to 'read between the lines' or **infer** the answer. You will have to form your own opinion from the clues in the text and scanning won't help you here. For example, to answer this kind of question you may need to:

- **predict**, or imagine, what happens, or might happen, next
- **give** your **opinion** about why a character does something or acts in a certain way
- **continue** the passage in your own words as a piece of writing (see Section C)

In order to infer, predict or continue, it is very important that you are clear about:

- **who** the characters are
- **where** and **when** the passage is taking place
- **what** is happening: the plot or the dilemma
- **why** the passage is worth reading.

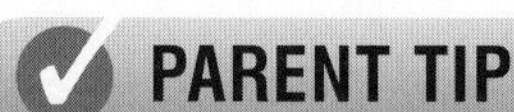

When reading to or with your child, be ready to discuss the meaning of the story or passage, bearing in mind the ***five Ws.***

Who? – There can be one or more main characters and less important characters. Try to spot clues that bring the characters to life so that you can imagine them as real people.

Where? When? – This is the setting and explains the place and the time of the passage. Again, use clues to imagine what kind of place it is and the time of day or season.

What? Why? – The events are what make the storyline or plot. The plot can include main events and minor ones. The dilemma or problem is often the cause of most events. Be clear about what is going on and why.

3 *Be aware of different text types*

Instructions tell you how to do something, like how to make a cup of tea. Instructions usually give step-by-step details which may be in bullet points or numbered lists.

Informative (explanatory) texts give facts about a topic, such as where tea comes from. These texts will usually have an introduction and will set out the facts clearly in paragraphs. They may also use some unfamiliar technical words and diagrams.

Descriptions describe a place, a person or a situation, such as what a tea plantation looks like. There may not be any characters or a plot, but just details.

Narrative texts tell a story. A narrative text has a plot that follows the experiences of the characters; for example, a story about workers on a tea plantation. It can be written in the first person, where characters tell their own story. If the narrator is not part of the story, it is written in the third person.

Poems are set out differently from prose (continuous writing). The lines are shorter and often begin with capital letters. Poems usually have a beat or a rhythm. Many have rhyming patterns.

Play scripts or film scripts are set out differently from poems or prose. The characters' names are written on the left-hand side of the page and are usually separated from their speech with a colon. A new line is used each time a different character speaks. The characters' movements (called stage directions) are written in brackets.

Can you work out what sort of text each of the following short extracts about water has come from?

a *The legend of El Dorado, the gilded one, grew rapidly after the Spaniards reached South America around 1500. High amongst the peaks of the Andes, in what is now Colombia, lay a crater which contained Lake Quatavita. Near the lake lived a peaceful people known as the Chibcha. Each new chief of the Chibcha celebrated his accession to kingship with a ceremony on the lake. The chief's body was covered in resinous gum and then a layer of gold dust. He was carried on a raft to the centre of the lake where he plunged into the water. His subjects and priests cast gold and precious stones such as emeralds into the lake.*

From *Buried Treasure* by Rupert Furneaux

This is an example of ______________________________

b Jack was away and up to his knees in the water in a moment, detaching the oysters. Ernest followed more leisurely, and, still unwilling to wet his feet, stood by the margin of the pool and gathered in his handkerchief the oysters his brother threw him; and as he thus stood he picked up and pocketed a large mussel-shell for his own use. As they returned with a good supply we heard a shout from Fritz in the distance; we returned it joyfully, and he presently appeared before us, his hands behind his back, and a look of disappointment upon his countenance.

"Unsuccessful!" said he.

"Really!" I replied; "never mind, my boy – better luck next time."

From *The Swiss Family Robinson* by J. D. Wyss

This is an example of ______________________________

c It is a fabulous place; when the tide is in, a wave-churned basin, creamy with foam, whipped by the combers that roll in from the whistling buoy on the reef. But when the tide goes out the little water world becomes quiet and lovely. The sea is very clear and the bottom becomes fantastic with hurrying, fighting, breeding animals. Crabs rush from frond to frond of the waving algae. Starfish squat over mussels and limpets, attach their million little suckers and then slowly lift with incredible power until the prey is broken from the rock.

From *Cannery Row* by John Steinbeck

This is an example of ______________________________

d ...And rushing and flushing and brushing and gushing,
And flapping and rapping and clapping and slapping,
And curling and whirling and purling and twirling,
And thumping and plumping and bumping and jumping,
And dashing and flashing and splashing and clashing;
And so never ending, but always descending,
Sounds and motions for ever and ever are blending,
All at once and all o'er, with a mighty uproar,
And this way the water comes down at Lodore.

From *The Cataract of Lodore* by Robert Southey

This is an example of ______________________________

e Pour some water in one beaker. Stick a blob of modelling clay to the end of the straw and float it in the beaker. Carefully mark on the straw the height that the water comes to. Fill the second beaker with salt solution and float your hydrometer in it. You will see that it does not sink as low as it does in water. Use cooking oil in the third beaker. This time the straw sinks lower than the water mark as oil is less dense than water.

From *How Science Works* by Judith Hann

This is an example of ______________________________

4 Check your answers

Most mistakes are made in the answers to the last questions in 11+ comprehension exercises, so check these extremely carefully! Try to remember these helpful hints when checking your answers:

Checklist

- ✓ look out for spellings, especially if any of the words you are using were in the passage
- ✓ be careful to punctuate accurately
- ✓ make sure the meaning of each answer is clear
- ✓ remember that there are clues in both the passage and the questions to help you answer correctly.

5 Practise the skills!

Now try the different types of comprehension exercises in this section and practise your skills.

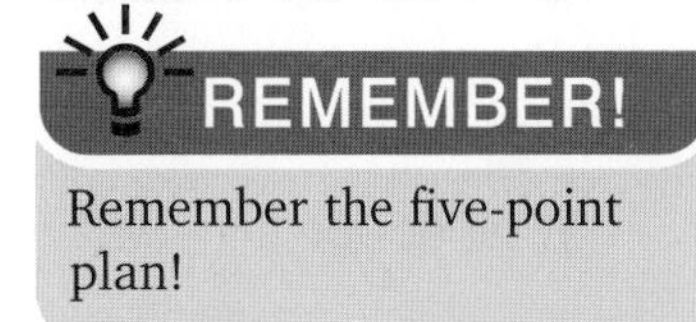
REMEMBER!
Remember the five-point plan!

A This is an example of a **narrative text** with a set of **standard** questions and a set of **multiple-choice** questions.

Tom lives with his younger brother Sid at their Aunt Polly's house. He has arranged a meeting with his friend Huckleberry Finn in the graveyard in the middle of the night.

At half past nine that night, Tom and Sid were sent to bed as usual. They said their prayers, and Sid was soon asleep. When it seemed to him that it must be nearly daylight, he heard the clock strike ten! This was despair. He would have tossed and fidgeted, as his nerves demanded, but he was afraid he might wake Sid. So he lay still and stared up into the dark. Everything was dismally still. By-and-by, out of the stillness little scarcely **perceptible** noises began to emphasise themselves. The ticking of the clock began to bring itself into notice. Old beams began to crack mysteriously. The stairs creaked faintly. Evidently spirits were abroad. A measured, muffled snore issued from Aunt Polly's chamber. And now the tiresome chirping of a cricket that no human ingenuity could **locate** began. Next the ghastly ticking of a death-watch in the wall at the bed's head made Tom shudder – it meant that somebody's days were numbered. Then the howl of a far-off dog rose on the night air and was answered by a fainter howl from a remoter distance. Tom was in an agony. At last he was satisfied that time had ceased and **eternity** begun; he began to doze in spite of himself; the clock chimed eleven, but he did not hear it. And then there came, **mingling** with his half-formed dreams, a most melancholy caterwauling. The raising of a neighbouring window disturbed him. A cry of "Scat! you devil!" and the crash of an empty bottle against the back of his aunt's wood-shed brought him wide awake, and a single minute later he was dressed and out of the window and creeping along the roof of the 'ell' on all fours.

From *Tom Sawyer* by Mark Twain

Standard

1 Explain why Tom was in despair. (2)

2 Make a list of seven sounds that Tom heard in the stillness. (7)

3 Why did hearing the death-watch beetle make Tom shudder? (2)

4 What do you think was happening when the empty bottle crashed? (2)

5 Think of another word or phrase that could be used instead of these words in bold print: (3)

A locate ______________ **B** eternity ______________ **C** mingling ______________

16

Have your answers marked. If you scored more than 12 out of 16, well done!

If you scored less than 12, think about these questions:

- Did you read the text, including the introduction, before starting to write?
- Did you read the questions carefully?
- Did you check how many points each question was worth?
- Did you scan the text for the answers?
- Did you answer the questions fully?
- Did you check your answers?
- Did you rush through the exercise?
- What did you find difficult?

Checking how many marks each question is worth can give you a hint about how much you need to write!

Look at the answers you got wrong and try to work out why. Practise comprehension exercises with standard questions.

Multiple-choice

Read through the text again, then underline each correct answer.

1 Tom wasn't able to move about at 10 o'clock because:

A his nerves were on edge **B** he was afraid of waking Sid

C he had been forbidden to toss and fidget **D** he was in despair

E he needed to wake Sid

2 In the passage, 'perceptible' means:

A easy to see **B** perceptive **C** recognisable **D** palpable **E** observable

3 Tom thought that there were spirits abroad because:

A small sounds made him think of ghosts **B** he had seen a ghost

C he had heard stories of ghosts in other countries

D a bottle of spirits had been left on the table **E** Aunt Polly was drunk

4 When the clock chimed 11:

A Tom was still awake **B** Sid was awake **C** it was the beginning of eternity

D Tom was caterwauling **E** Tom was sleeping lightly

5 In the passage, 'mingling' means:

A tingling **B** interfering **C** mixing **D** struggling **E** competing

6 The person who cried "Scat! you devil!" was:

A Tom **B** Sid **C** Aunt Polly **D** a drunkard **E** a neighbour

7 There were two howls in the night. One was a dog. The other was:

A the dog next door **B** a wolf **C** an echo **D** another dog's distant response

E the dog who first howled, now locked up

8 '…the tiresome chirping of a cricket that no human ingenuity could locate' means:

A Tom had lost his cricket bat **B** Tom was fed up with playing cricket

C Tom kept a pet cricket and it was lost

D it was impossible for anyone to find the cricket by using its sound

E it was ingenious the way crickets made people tired

8

Have your work marked, with one point for each correct answer. If you scored more than six out of eight, well done!

If you scored less than six, think about these questions:

- Did you read the text in full first?
- Did you read the questions and possible answers carefully?
- Did you scan the text for each question?
- Did you rush through the exercise?
- What did you find difficult?

REMEMBER!

Look for options that do not make sense and you can cross out straight away. This will make it easier to choose the correct answer.

Look at the answers you got wrong and try to work out why. Practise comprehension exercises with multiple-choice questions.

You could be asked to continue this story in your own words, taking half an hour or so, for the writing part of your exam.

Have a go!

Have your story checked and use the advice in Section C to help you with story writing.

B This is an example of a comprehension exercise where the text is a **poem**. The questions are a mixture of **standard** and **multiple-choice**.

The Fawn

There it was I saw what I shall never forget
And never retrieve.
Monstrous and beautiful to human eyes, hard to believe,
He lay, yet there he lay,
Asleep on the moss, his head on his polished ***cleft*** *small ebony hooves,*
The child of the doe, the ***dappled*** *child of the deer.*

Surely his mother had never said, "Lie here
Till I return," so spotty and plain to see
On the green moss lay he.
His eyes had opened; he considered me.

I would have given more than I care to say
To thrifty ears, might I have had him for my friend
One moment only of that forest day:

Might I have had the acceptance, not the love
Of those clear eyes;
Might I have been for him the bough above
Or the root beneath his forest bed,
A part of the forest, seen without surprise.

Was it alarm, or was it the wind of my fear lest he depart
That jerked him to his jointy knees,
And sent him crashing off, leaping and stumbling
On his new legs, between the stems of the white trees?

Edna St Vincent Millay, published 1934

1 Find three different details about the fawn from different verses. (3)

____

____

2 Why does the poet think the doe cannot have left the fawn in that place deliberately? (1)

____

____

3 How long would the poet have liked to be friends with the fawn? (1)

____

____

4 Which three-word phrase explains how the poet would have liked to have been looked at by the fawn? (3)

____

____

5 Which three verbs explain the movement of the fawn as it leaves? (3)

____

____

6 Find the three words from the poem which make rhyming pairs with these words: (3)

A believe ____________ **B** trees ____________ **C** love ____________

7 Underline the best meaning from the choices for these words in the poem: (2)

cleft:	sharp	split	clever	dirty	new
dapped:	sunlit	pretty	shaded	spotted	camouflaged

16

How did you do? If you scored 12 or more out of 16, well done!

If you scored less than 12, check which questions let you down. Try to work out why by asking yourself some of the questions listed below each section in exercise A.

C This comprehension exercise uses a piece of **informative/explanatory** text.

Hammerhead Sharks

Of all the sharks, hammerheads have the strangest shaped heads. Included in the nine species of hammerhead are the bonnetheads, which have only small head projections. The winged hammerhead has by far the widest head, which can be half as long as its body. Most hammerhead species live in warm temperate and tropical coastal waters. The scalloped hammerhead is one of the most common species and occurs in warm waters throughout the world. Large schools of scalloped hammerheads congregate in some areas where there are features on the sea floor like undersea peaks or sea mounts. A hundred of these sharks may form a school with them all swimming in **unison**. At dusk they swim off on their own to feed and then at dawn they regroup in the same place.

From *Shark, Eyewitness Guides* by Miranda MacQuitty

1 Name three different types of hammerhead shark mentioned in this passage. (3)

____

____

2 How many species of hammerhead are there? (1)

____

____

3 In which two habitats do hammerheads generally live? (2)

____

____

4 Name two features of the scalloped hammerheads' favourite gathering places. (2)

____

____

5 What is extraordinary about the winged hammerhead's size? (1)

____

____

6 Explain the word **unison** in the passage. (1)

____

____

7 Which sort of hammerhead is commonly found worldwide in warm waters? (1)

____

____

8 Scalloped hammerheads feed alone: (1)

A at night **B** when it is cloudy **C** when the light fades **D** at sunrise **E** at midnight

9 Find single words in the passage that mean: (4)

A a group of sharks ______________ **B** sticking-out bumps ______________

C first light ______________ **D** assemble ______________

16

How did you do? If you scored 12 or more out of 16, well done!

If you scored less than 12, work out why, learn from your mistakes and keep practising!

D This is an example of a comprehension test using **instructions**. The questions are all **multiple-choice**. Underline each correct answer.

Painted Pots

You will need: a clean terracotta plant pot; tracing paper; masking tape; a broad-edged paint brush from an art supplier's; an old jar lid; carbon paper; two pencils; scrap paper.

1 Make sure the surface of the pot is **absolutely** clean. If you need to wash it, leave it overnight to dry, as this type of pot absorbs a lot of water.
2 To see how long the pattern should be, cut a strip of tracing paper to fit around the pot. Try some patterns on **scrap** paper. You could try using two pencils. Tape them together. Have the pencil points **level**.
3 Once you are happy with your design, trace it onto the strip of tracing paper. Tape a piece of carbon paper onto the pot, inky side down, then tape the tracing paper over it.
4 Use a hard pencil to trace over the outline of your pattern. The carbon paper will **transfer** the pattern as lines onto your pot.
5 On a lid, mix some acrylic paint with water so that it is like thin cream. Paint over the pattern with the brush. Some shades may need two coats.

From *The Usborne Book of Making Presents* by Ray Gibson

1 You can get a broad-edged paint brush from:

A a hardware store **B** your school **C** an artist friend **D** an art supplier's **E** a paintbox

2 Terracotta pots:

A are made out of plastic **B** soak up water easily **C** need to be washed

D have dirty surfaces **E** are good water containers

3 The old jar lid is for:

A keeping the pot dry **B** making patterns **C** storing the tape

D trying out designs **E** mixing paint with water

4 You have the carbon paper with its inky side down so that:

A the pattern is transferred onto the pot **B** your fingers don't get inky

C the tape doesn't get inky **D** the pattern is easier to trace

E the ink and paint don't mix

5 Using a pair of pencils taped together will:

A make a darker mark **B** make the pencil points level **C** make a double pattern

D be useful if one breaks **E** help to make a fun design

6 You may have to paint on two coats if:

A it is cold **B** you use a brush **C** the cream is too thin

D you are wearing sunglasses **E** the colour of the paint is pale

7 Choose the most appropriate word that could be substituted for the words in bold from the passage:

absolutely:	fairly	reasonably	absurdly	completely	suitably
scrap:	squared	lined	discarded	rough	damaged
level:	lined-up	staggered	horizontal	vertical	oblique
transfer:	erase	remove	imitate	copy	etch

(4)

10

Each correct answer scores one point. How did you do? If you scored seven or more out of 10, well done!

If you scored less than seven, think about where you went wrong and keep practising!

E This is a comprehension exercise where the text is part of a **play script**. The questions are all in a standard format.

Ant's Pants

(Characters: **Anthony** and **Marlon**, 12-year-old boys)

(Anthony and Marlon enter. They are in the centre of town. Marlon is obviously very bored.)

Marlon: Why did we have to come shopping?
Ant: Because I need a new shirt for the school disco on Friday.
Marlon: You're not going to that, are you?
Ant: Why not?
Marlon: It's rubbish! All the teachers bouncing about in their flower-power **gear**, trying to get you to dance with them, and old Fungus Williams, playing his **ancient** records. 'Do-wah-diddy-diddy-dum-diddy-do.' It's **pathetic**!
Ant: You don't like school discos **'cos** your mum turned up at the last one at nine o'clock to take you home, and Fungus announced it over the **mike**.
Marlon: **Yeah**, well it was embarrassing.
Ant: Anyway, I'm going. I've been practising this **mega** dance routine. Everybody is going to be well impressed!
Marlon: Bighead!
Ant: Oh yeah? Watch this!
Marlon: Not here, Ant. You'll show me up!
Ant: Stand back and marvel!

(Ant begins to hum one of the latest hit sounds and starts to move in time to it. His dancing gets wilder and wilder.)

Ant: And now for the best bit!

(He leaps up in the air and comes down in the 'splits' position. There is a loud ripping noise.)

Ant: Oh no!
Marlon: What's the matter?
Ant: I've split my jeans!
Marlon (bursting into laughter): Serves you right, you bighead!

From *Ant's Pants* by Steve Barlow and Steve Skidmore, in *The Oxford English Programme 1*

1 Why are the two boys in town? (1)

____

____

2 What does Marlon think about school discos? (1)

____

____

3 What happened at the last one to make him think like this? (2)

____

____

4 When Marlon says 'Do-wah-diddy-diddy-dum-diddy-do', what does he mean? (1)

____

____

5 Why is Ant looking forward to the school disco? (1)

____

____

6 Find another word or phrase that could be used instead of each of these words: (4)

A ancient ________ **B** pathetic ________ **C** mega ________ **D** gear ________

7 What are the parts of the text that are printed in brackets? (1)

____

____

8 What do these three shortened words stand for?: (3)

A 'cos ________ **B** mike ________ **C** yeah ________

9 Why do you think the three shortened words have been used instead of the words they stand for? (1)

____

____

10 Marlon calls Ant a 'bighead' twice. Why? (1)

____

____

16

How did you do? If you scored 12 or more out of 16, well done.

If you scored less than 12, learn from your mistakes and keep practising!

Use the range of Bond Assessment Papers in English *and* Bond 11+ Test Papers in English *to give your child more comprehension practice.*

C Writing

Most 11+ English exams will require you to show your writing skills and your ideas in a creative way. This could be called:

- a composition
- a story
- an essay
- a description.

It is difficult to say how many titles you will be given to choose from for this part of the exam. Sometimes you will have one or two titles; sometimes there will be a whole set of different options.

You may have to:

- write a factual essay such as 'My Hobbies' or 'My Family'
- write a letter
- read a short beginning and then finish the story yourself
- answer questions on a comprehension passage and then continue writing the passage as a writing test.

You always have a certain time to produce your writing. This could be between 30 minutes and one hour. Read the instructions at the beginning carefully, so that you know how much time you have. Then, remember to keep an eye on the time as you write.

"Why do I have to write something?"

Creative writing gives you a chance to shine. You can show off your:

- wide reading
- creativeness
- knowledge of what makes writing special
- extensive vocabulary
- enjoyment of language
- fluency

PARENT TIP

Make sure your child understands what each of these means. You can really support him or her by pointing out these aspects of his or her work.

To start with, let's think about writing stories. The other main kinds of writing will be dealt with later on in Section 7 (page 44).

1 *Learn how to plan stories*

Getting started is often the most challenging part!

That's where noting down a short plan can be very helpful. It will help you to **organise** your ideas and give your writing a **structure**.

First of all, think about these tips:

Checklist

- Remember that you're going to write a short story, essay or description, not a book!
- Keep your ideas simple.
- Always bear the title and instructions in mind.
- Think about who is going to tell (narrate) the story. You? Or one of the characters?

Next, using bullet points and key words, you could jot down:

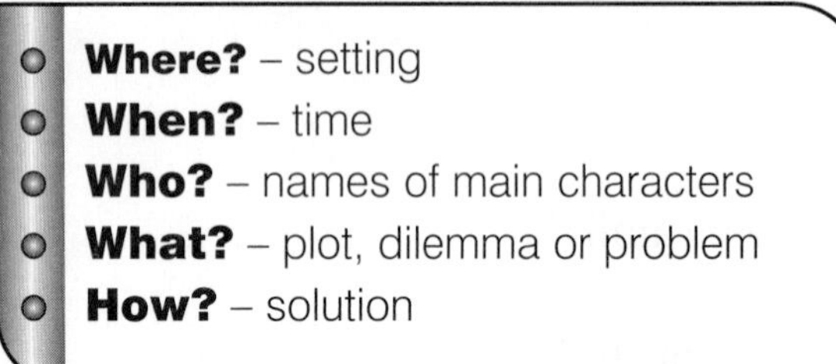

- **Where?** – setting
- **When?** – time
- **Who?** – names of main characters
- **What?** – plot, dilemma or problem
- **How?** – solution

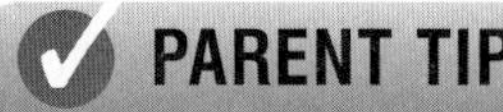

Make up or find stories for which your child can think of answers to these questions. This is a good game to do orally in the car!

"I don't like planning. I just want to write."

Everyone's different; some people really find it cramps their style to plan, and like to go with the flow of writing. That's fine, as long as you keep the structure or shape of your story going: **beginning**, **middle**, **end**. (Jump to Section 2, *Learn how to write stories*, if you don't want to practise planning.)

For those of you who find it helpful to plan, the next stage of planning concerns **paragraphs**. These are the 'chunks' or 'stages' of your writing and, if you forget to use them, it is very difficult to do anything about it by the time you reach the checking stage. So, part of your planning needs to develop your story in paragraphs, using bullet points to remind yourself of key words.

For instance, given the title 'Tunnel Adventure', you could:

1 First, plan a rough outline like this:

- **Where?** – rocky seaside
- **When?** – summer holidays
- **Who?** – Ed and Joe, brothers
- **What?** – explore, find tunnel, nearly get caught in rising tide
- **How?** – swim to safety

2 Next, develop the plot in paragraphs:

- explore rock pools
- tunnel leads to possible treasure or pirates
- notice rising tide
- time is running out.

...or whatever you decide.

This should remind you to begin a new paragraph for each new stage of your story. Of course, if there is dialogue, each time someone starts talking you also need to start a new paragraph.

"I find planning difficult."

Many people do: you are not alone! It's easy to practise, though, and practice will make you more aware of sorting out your planning and keeping it brief.

Set yourself five minutes to write a short plan for a story called: 'A Day to Remember':

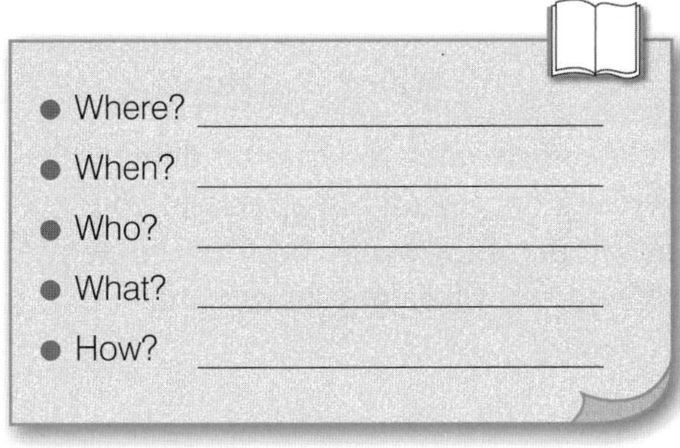
- Where? ______________________
- When? ______________________
- Who? ______________________
- What? ______________________
- How? ______________________

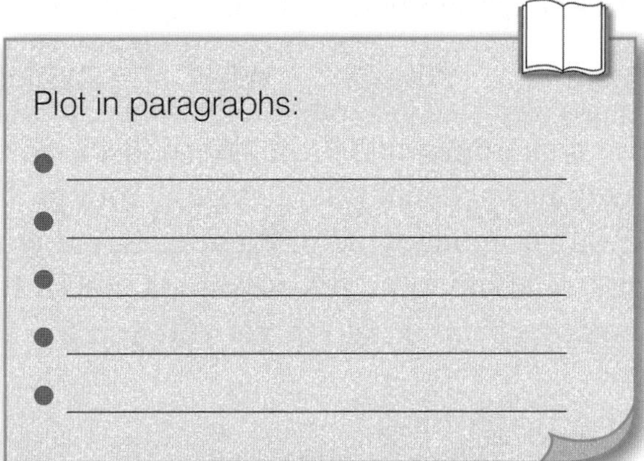
Plot in paragraphs:
- ______________________
- ______________________
- ______________________
- ______________________
- ______________________

When you have finished, discuss your plans with someone else. Have the plans given a **shape** and **structure** to a possible piece of writing?

PARENT TIP

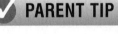

First give positive comments on the plans; then offer constructive suggestions for possible improvements.

Here are some more examples of story titles. Have a go at writing plans for each of them in five minutes. When you have finished, discuss them with other people.

'Problems with Pets' **'Look Before you Leap'** **'What a Relief!'**

2 *Learn how to write stories*

It's down to business! You have learnt and practised how to plan your story. Now you need to start writing.

What are your **aims** when writing a story?

Checklist

- ✓ **Think** about the title or the instructions – before you begin writing, as you are writing and when you check at the end.
- ✓ **Structure** your story. It needs a beginning, a middle and an end.
- ✓ **Organise** your story in sentences and paragraphs.
- ✓ **Entertain** your reader. There's no point writing something so boring it sends your reader to sleep!
- ✓ **Communicate** what you want to say to your reader clearly. Your spelling, grammar and punctuation must be accurate.
- ✓ **Write** legibly. Your reader needs to be able to read what you have written.

Recall these aims whenever you are giving feedback on writing. It can be hard for people to stand back from their own writing and remember these key aims.

Bear these aims in mind when you do any writing.

"But I can't think of anything to write."

Writer's block

Writer's block is a very common problem, not just for children preparing for exams. Planning should help you get started, but if you're still stuck, try the **'w w w w w w h'** trick. Each letter stands for a question word:

Where? **When?** **Why?** **Which?** **Who?** **What?** **How?**

It's sometimes called the 'journalist's trick', as journalists have to write on demand to keep newspapers full of stories. You, too, are writing on demand in an exam. You thought about some of these question words at the planning stage, but they come in useful at any time when you get stuck. Just ask yourself these questions; your answers should help to get you going.

The beginning

You must try to grab your reader's attention from the very start, so welcome your reader in! You could think about how to:

Checklist

- ✓ set the scene
- ✓ introduce at least one character
- ✓ give some hints about a problem that the characters will face later
- ✓ use interesting language to describe the scene and characters
- ✓ plunge into the story.

Get stuck into the story and try to enjoy it! The chances are then your reader will too.

1 Look at the first paragraph in a range of books. See how the authors cope with beginning a story.

- Do they grab your attention?
- Do you want to go on reading?
- Do you get an idea of what the story will be like?
- Is it clear who is telling the story?

Find a collection of short stories and see how these begin.

2 Now it's your turn! Have a go at writing an opening paragraph for each of the titles you planned:

- 'A Day to Remember'
- 'Problems with Pets'
- 'Look Before you Leap'
- 'What a Relief!'

Ask someone to read your introductions and give you feedback.

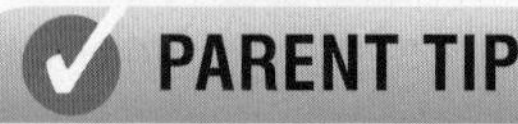

Be positive!
Be constructive!

The middle

This is where the action happens, so keep up the pace. Remember, your time is limited!

The middle of the story could:

Checklist

- ✓ contain all the main parts of the plot
- ✓ uncover the dilemma or problem
- ✓ explore the different personalities of the characters

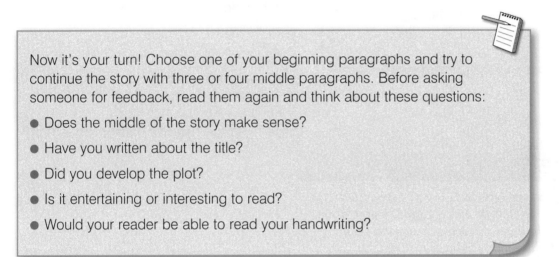

You need to write in paragraphs and your plan can help remind you. If you use dialogue, each time a different character starts talking, you need a new paragraph.

You are telling the story. You are the master magician and the pen is your wand!

Now it's your turn! Choose one of your beginning paragraphs and try to continue the story with three or four middle paragraphs. Before asking someone for feedback, read them again and think about these questions:

- Does the middle of the story make sense?
- Have you written about the title?
- Did you develop the plot?
- Is it entertaining or interesting to read?
- Would your reader be able to read your handwriting?

The End

"I just write 'The End'."

This is where you bring your story to a close. It should be quite clear to your reader that your story has come to an end, so there's no need to write 'The End'.

For the ending of your story, which may be only one paragraph, you could:

Checklist

- ✓ find a solution for the dilemma or problem
- ✓ tie up loose ends – unless you want to leave your reader guessing by using a cliffhanger
- ✓ perhaps refer back to the title in some way, or explain the moral of the story, if there is one.

1 Look at the final paragraph in a range of books. See how the authors cope with ending a book.

- Have the authors solved all the problems?
- Do any endings leave you guessing?
- How do the endings make you feel?

Find a collection of short stories and see how these end.

2 Now it's your turn! Write an ending for your beginning and middle paragraphs. Before asking someone for some feedback, read your final paragraphs again and think about these questions:

- Have you written a satisfying ending?
- Does it tie up all the loose ends?
- Is it clear that this is the end of your story?
- Does it refer back to the title?
- How do you want your reader to feel at the end?

PARENT TIP

Advise your child to avoid endings such as: 'It was all a dream' or: 'They all lived happily ever after'. It may be helpful to discuss clichés at this point!

3 *Check your writing*

All writers need to check what they have written. Professional writers pay proofreaders to do this job for them. You will have to check your work yourself, so always make sure you leave time to check your writing at the end.

It is important to keep at least five minutes of your writing time for checking. Practise reading out your writing to yourself sentence by sentence. That way you can learn to check the first three most vital parts of this checklist:

Checklist

- ✓ **sense**
- ✓ **sentences**
- ✓ **spelling**
- ✓ punctuation
- ✓ grammar
- ✓ interest
- ✓ vocabulary
- ✓ handwriting

PARENT TIP

Practise checking through one or two stories together. Ask your child to read them aloud sentence by sentence, so that he or she gets the hang of this.

Use the checklist to go through the stories you have practised writing so far.

④ *Improve your writing*

You have learnt and practised how to give your writing a clear structure by planning and writing a beginning, a middle and an end. You have also thought about how to check your story. It is now time to think about how to improve your story-writing in more detail.

Have a look at these four examples of children's writing. The children were shown this short picture story and asked to write an interesting and entertaining sentence for each picture. This isn't the type of exercise you will be given in an 11+ English exam, but it is very useful for recognising different kinds of story-writing.

based on 'Greedy Mouse' from *Picture Stories* by Rodney Peppé

A

one day creedy mouse was very hungry so he went to look for some food. He found a peice of ceses on the flor. He ate some then he ate it all. and could not get back in his hole.

by Lily

This story has a beginning, a middle and an end. But it is very dull! You could call it a 'bare bones' story. It has all the structure, but is not entertaining or interesting for the reader. What could be done about improving a story like this?

Here's a different version of the same story.

B

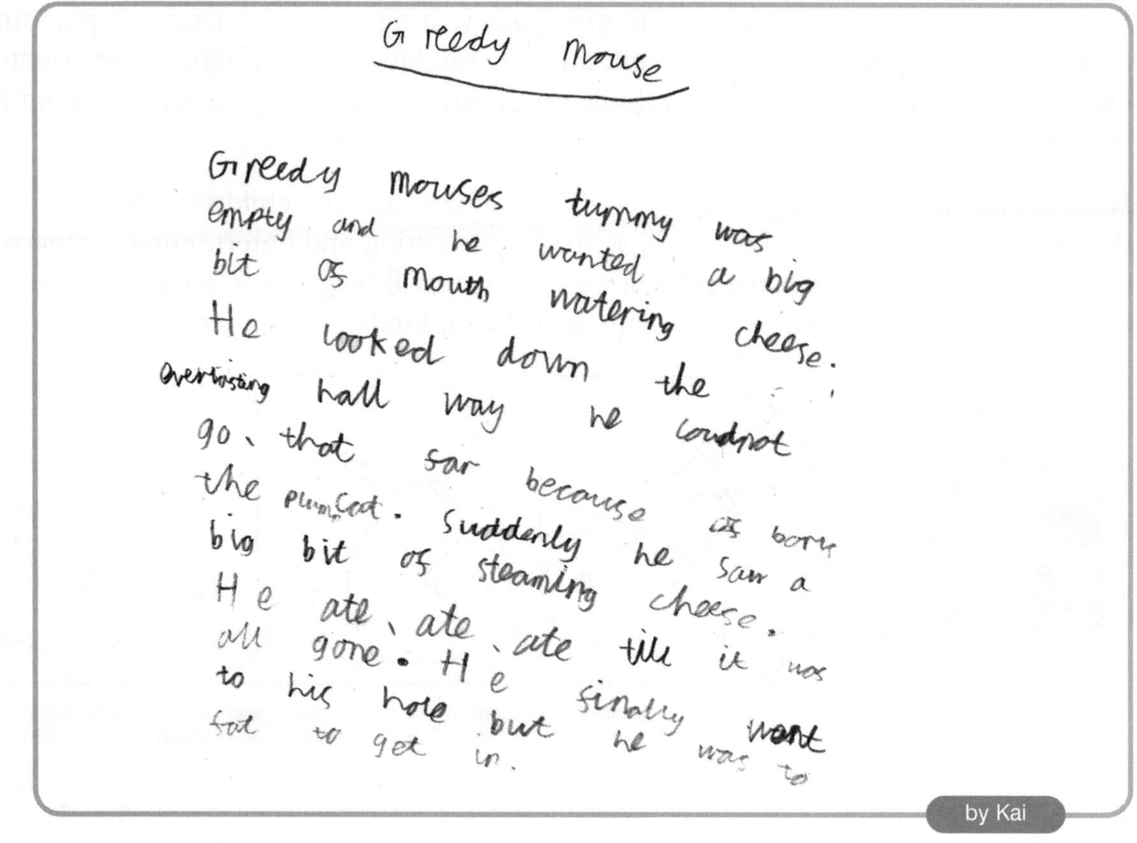

Greedy mouse

Greedy mouses tummy was empty and he wanted a big bit of mouth watering cheese. He looked down the overlasting hall way he coudnot go that far because of the plumcat. Suddenly he saw a big bit of steaming cheese. He ate, ate, ate till it was all gone. He finally went to his hole but he was to fat to get in.

by Kai

You can see that Kai has developed the 'bare bones' writing that Lily produced by adding details, humour and more interesting vocabulary.

C Here is a third version of the same story.

Greedy Mouse

1 Greedy Mouse was really hungry, as the hog family never left any crumbs at dinner.

2 "Hey look at that enormous piece of cheese!" Greedy Mouse thought out loud.

3 "Mmmm, yum yum, yum," thought greedy mouse, "that was delicious!"

4 "Oh, no, now I can't get into my hole, but hey, at least there's that lump of cheese I haven't yet polished off!"

by Annabel

Here you can see that Annabel has added not only details, humour and interesting vocabulary, but also dialogue.

D Finally, this version is developed even further.

The scrowley grey mouse was as ravenous as a street child.

He was scavenging for food about the castle when he came across the most mouth watering piece of cheese he had ever seen in his life

In a split second he had eaten almost all of it like a vulture feeding on a dead elephant.

He was just finnishing the last bit when he let out a humungous yawn so he waddled off to bed, but he had eaten so much that he could no longer fit through his mouse hole! he squeesed his head throug his tummy

by Sophie

Sophie has really developed her vocabulary, by adding adjectives, details and similes, using complex sentences and thinking about the mouse's feelings.

You can make your writing more interesting too by using some or all of these ideas:

Checklist

- ✓ bring your characters to life (page 30)
- ✓ add details (page 31)
- ✓ think about feelings (page 32)
- ✓ use adjectives and adverbs (page 33)
- ✓ develop your vocabulary (page 34)
- ✓ vary your sentences (page 35)
- ✓ include dialogue (page 37)
- ✓ add imagery (page 38)
- ✓ think about the senses (page 41)
- ✓ write clearly and legibly. (page 42)

"I've forgotten how to do these things."

In the next section, each of the ideas in the checklist above is described in more detail. Read through any that you are unsure about and do the exercises for practice.

Bring your characters to life

Including just a few details about your characters can help your reader to imagine them more clearly. Try making a flow chart about a character like this:

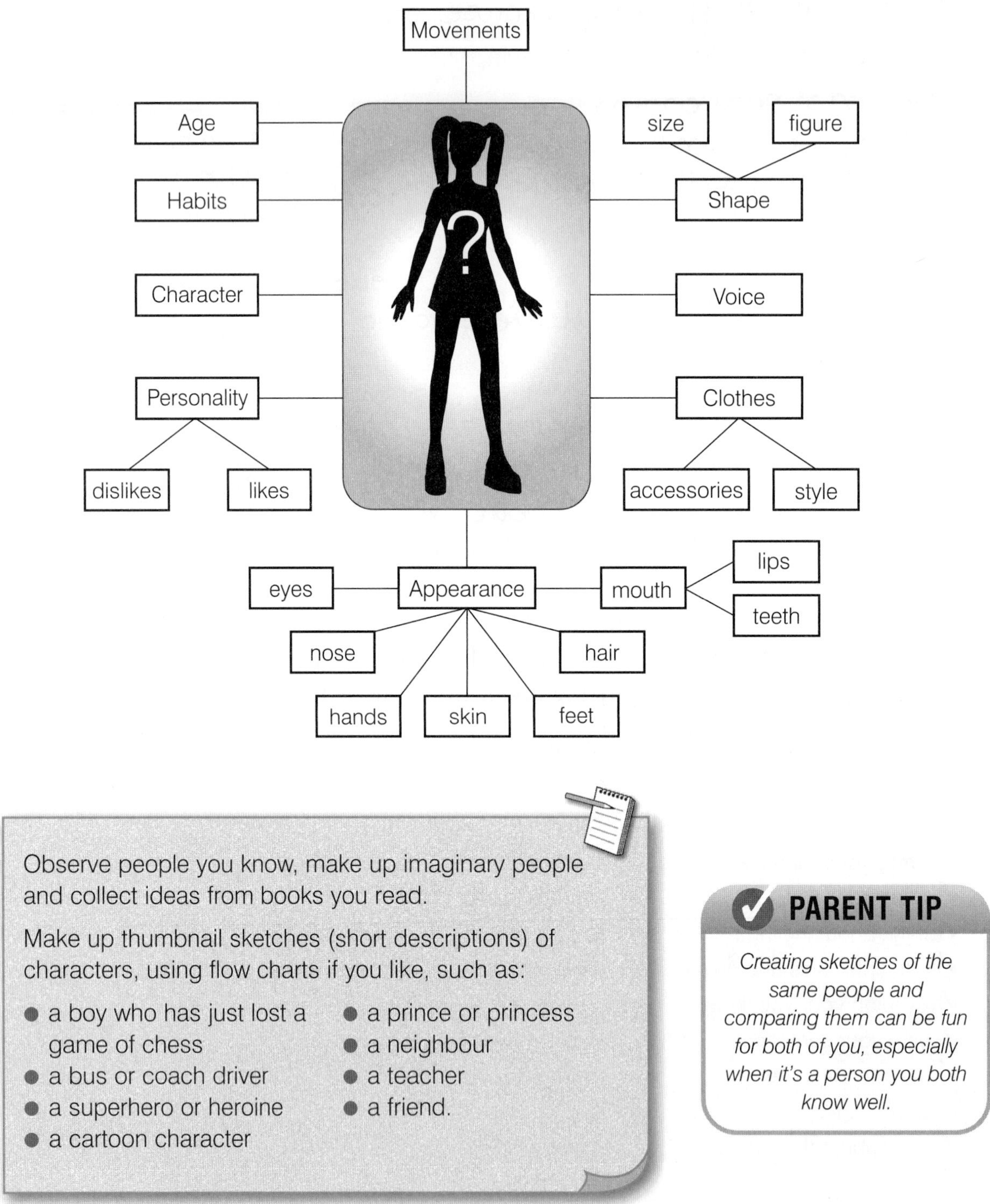

Observe people you know, make up imaginary people and collect ideas from books you read.

Make up thumbnail sketches (short descriptions) of characters, using flow charts if you like, such as:

- a boy who has just lost a game of chess
- a bus or coach driver
- a superhero or heroine
- a cartoon character
- a prince or princess
- a neighbour
- a teacher
- a friend.

PARENT TIP

Creating sketches of the same people and comparing them can be fun for both of you, especially when it's a person you both know well.

A useful exercise is to write two completely different sketches of the same character. This will help to show how different details can change the mood, personality and appearance of a character. Your reader will have a different opinion of the character, too.

For instance, compare these two descriptions:

1 *Chris shrugged his shoulders gloomily after his defeat, his lank hair drooping over his sullen eyes. "I never seem to win," he muttered.*

2 *Chris's entire face beamed, in spite of his disappointing defeat. "It was a brilliant game, even though I lost," he laughed, his black eyes sparkling through his mop of hair.*

Notice how what Chris says helps to show his personality. Also notice how the details of what Chris looks like change the way you think about him.

Add details

When you are writing, you could just write a 'bare bones' story, which has all the parts that make up a story (a beginning, a middle and an end) but is like a tree in winter or a fleshless skeleton. A 'bare bones' story is not likely to entertain or grab the attention of the reader. You would not really be using your imagination, either.

Compare these two versions of the same story. The second version shows how a 'bare bones' story can be developed not just by adding adjectives and adverbs, but also through using phrases to make more complex, more interesting and more informative sentences.

1 *The bird hopped onto the path. He pecked for crumbs. Billy the cat was watching him. Suddenly the cat pounced. The bird just managed to fly away. Billy had a feather trapped under his paw.*

2 *Swooping down from its apple-tree perch, the bird, a sparrow, hopped confidently onto the gravelled garden path. He pecked left and right for crumbs, his head bobbing, his bright eyes alert and attentive.*

In the gloom beneath the holly bush, Billy, the marmalade tomcat, was hunched, tense, coiled like a tight spring, his tail rigid and his pale yellow eyes watching the bird.

Suddenly, like a cannonball, the cat pounced, landing on the gravel with a scrunch. Simultaneously, the bird jerked into the air with a thin screech and a flurry of feathers and just managed to fly away.

Billy, arranging himself into a sitting position, his eyes narrowed in disappointment, had a tiny pale brown feather trapped beneath his left paw.

1 Using a highlighter pen, mark the parts in the second description that are the 'bare bones' of the first version. Notice the changes and the kinds of details that have been added to the second version.

1 a What extra information is given about the bird in the second version of the story?

b What does the first version of the story **not** tell you about Billy?

c Which version did you find more interesting to read? Can you say why?

2 Look out for how different authors develop ideas in your reading. Make a note of your favourite descriptions. Try taking some of the words away to see how this affects the scenes.

Practise adding details to these short scenes in a similar way:

- A man runs to catch a bus but misses it.
- A dog digs for a bone and gets stung by a wasp.
- A child swings too high and falls off the swing.

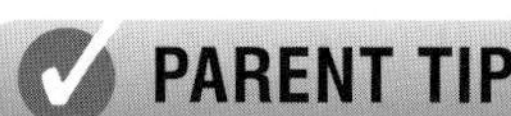

Develop some 'bare bones' situations together. You can do this orally.

Think about feelings

Here are some examples of ways we can feel from time to time:

angry   delighted   jealous   excited   sorry

disappointed   sad   frightened   anxious   lonely   happy

It is easy to forget about including feelings when you are writing. Using them can help your characters to come alive. After all, different people react in different ways to things that happen.

You can collect many ideas by observing yourself and others in real life, as well as in books, films or plays.

For instance, feeling **angry** can make you:

Checklist

- ✓ see red
- ✓ want to explode
- ✓ shout and scream
- ✓ hide
- ✓ jump up and down
- ✓ say things you don't mean
- ✓ cry
- ✓ stamp your feet
- ✓ slam doors.

1 Choose two or three of the feelings listed above. Write a short paragraph about when you experienced them.

Jot down some ways in which you and your body react when you feel some of these emotions.

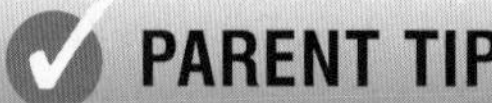

You could discuss with your child how he or she reacts emotionally in different situations. This can be quite revealing!

2 Make a collection of ways in which authors describe their characters' feelings which you particularly like and think you could use in your own writing.

Here are some things to think about:

- Have different authors described the same feeling in different ways?
- Would you have felt and reacted the same as the characters in these situations?
- How would you have described these feelings?

Use adjectives and adverbs

Every sentence, even the most basic, needs a subject and a verb. The subject can be:

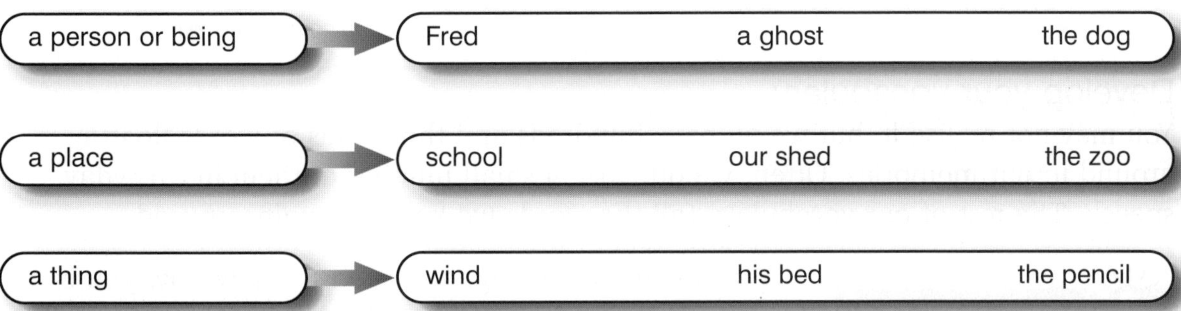

To make a simple sentence from these subjects you can add a verb:

Fred **jumped**. A ghost **appeared**. The dog **barked**.
School **starts**. Our shed **collapsed**. The zoo **opened**.
Wind **whistles**. His bed **creaked**. The pencil **snapped**.

As you can see, these sentences are so basic that they are pretty dull!

By **ad**ding **ad**jectives or **ad**verbs you can transform them in any way you like.

Old Fred jumped **carefully**. An **eerie** ghost appeared **suddenly**.
The **anxious** dog barked **frantically**. His **rickety** bed creaked **alarmingly**.

And so on…

Adjectives and adverbs add detail to the subject or object you are describing. By using them you can vary simple sentences in countless ways. So, if you include different adjectives and adverbs in your writing, you will make a story much more effective, vivid and attention-grabbing for the reader. (See Section D6, page 60, for more information on adjectives and adverbs.)

1 Choose a short descriptive passage in one of your books. Look out for places where the author has included adjectives and adverbs.

- Make a list of adjectives and adverbs in the passage.
- What types of things do they help to describe?
- Rewrite the passage without the adjectives and adverbs. Is the passage still as enjoyable to read?

2 Build collections of interesting adjectives and adverbs you can use in your writing. Sort them by type so they are easier to remember. For example, arrange them in columns under these headings:

Size Shape Age Number Emotion Colour

*A good game is to find adjectives to go with animals in alphabetical order, e.g.: an **a**lert **a**ardvark; a **b**oastful **b**ear; a **c**unning **c**heetah, etc.*

Develop your vocabulary

You may not realise it, but we all have hundreds and thousands of words floating around in our memories. Often, we only use a small number of them in everyday speech. The rest of our vocabulary (all the words we know) remains unused.

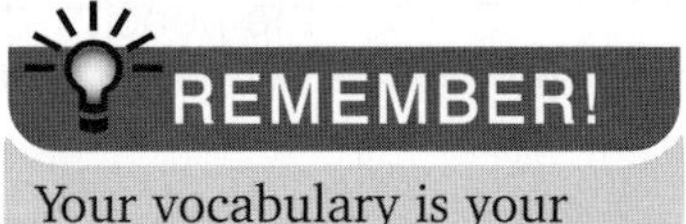

Your vocabulary is your word power!

When you are writing, you need to show how you can choose appropriate words to build up a clear picture of what you want to say. This can make your writing more original and individual. What you want to say, and how you say it, is likely to be very different from what someone else would write.

Be interested in words!

The world around you is packed with words, so try to 'soak up' as many as you can! Here are some ways you can learn new words:

Checklist

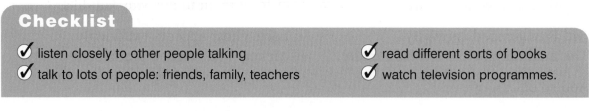

- ✓ listen closely to other people talking
- ✓ talk to lots of people: friends, family, teachers
- ✓ read different sorts of books
- ✓ watch television programmes.

You can even learn new words while playing computer games!

A **dictionary** and a **thesaurus** are also wonderful places to find out about words.

Use a thesaurus to search for alternative versions of the most common or simple words that first spring to mind. Words that have the same or similar meanings are called **synonyms**. (See Section D9, page 65, for more detail on synonyms.) Using synonyms in your writing can help to avoid repetition. This can make a story more descriptive and more interesting for the reader.

One of the most common and overused words in English is the word 'said'. A quick look in a thesaurus shows that there are many interesting alternatives that can be used instead. (You may need to look up 'to say' as 'said' is the past tense of this verb.)

For instance:

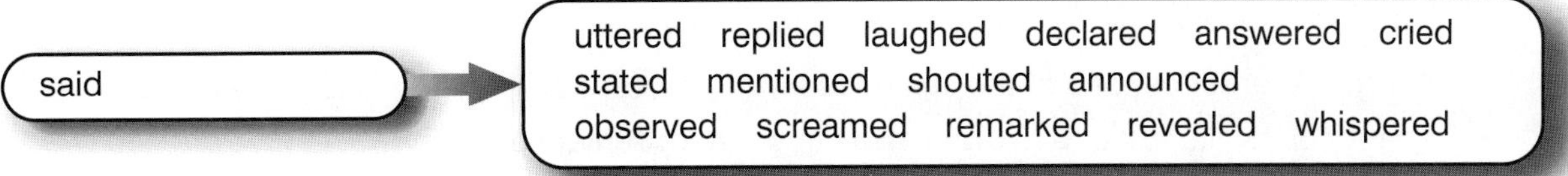

said
uttered replied laughed declared answered cried
stated mentioned shouted announced
observed screamed remarked revealed whispered

Be brave! Try out new words in your writing but make sure you know what they mean, and how they are spelt, so that you can use them accurately.

1 Make a 'juicy words' page in your exercise book. Collect words and phrases you like the sound of and could use in your own writing.

PARENT TIP

Take it in turns to find synonyms for some common words. How long can you keep going?

2 Draw six columns in your exercise book. Write one of these common words at the top of each column:

little big went nice lots then

Build up a collection of possible alternatives (synonyms) for these and other common words.

Try to think about alternatives when writing stories.

Vary your sentences

Ben plodded home from school. Then he went upstairs. Then he got out his Lego. Then he played with it. Then he had his meal. Then he went to bed.

We all used to write like this when we were first learning to write. All our sentences had the same shape and most began in the same way. You can see these are not very exciting sentences to read.

Understanding how to change the shape and length of sentences in different ways is an important skill that you need to show in your writing. Using a variety of sentences can help to make your writing more interesting for your reader.

You can transform sentences in all kinds of ways. You can:

Checklist

- ✓ add adjectives or adverbs
- ✓ use connectives (or conjunctions) to join two or more short sentences together
- ✓ add phrases of time or place to the beginning or end
- ✓ change the order of parts of the sentence
- ✓ use pronouns like **who**, **which** or **that** to connect sentences.

See how the first sentences from the story about Ben could be transformed:

Nine-year-old Ben plodded **wearily** home from school.

Ben plodded home from school **and** went upstairs.
or
Ben plodded home from school, went upstairs, got out his Lego **and** played with it.

At half past three, Ben plodded home from school, **past** the playing field.

Ben went **upstairs** after he plodded home from school.

Ben, **who** was really tired, plodded home from school, which seemed a long way.

1 Have a go at rewriting the story about Ben, varying all the sentences. How many different versions can you make?

2 Here are some simple sentences for you to try transforming. Try using the different ways described in the list above.

- Then Carly heard a scream.
- It was a sunny morning.
- We had lunch at half past twelve.
- Ishmal was drawing. His pencil broke. He got a new one from the drawer.

PARENT TIP

Here's another useful car journey game! Take it in turns to transform or expand the same sentence.

Include dialogue

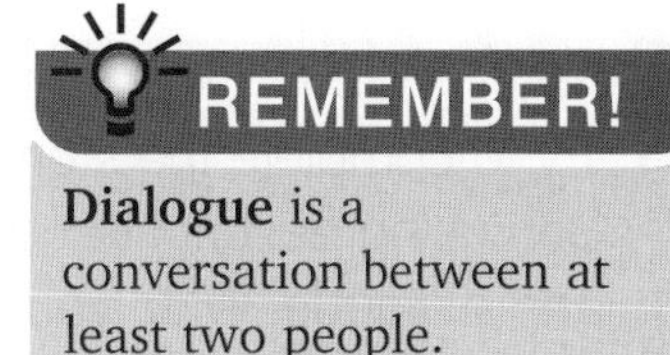

Dialogue is a conversation between at least two people.

By including dialogue (direct speech) in your stories, you write down some of what your characters actually say. Using dialogue can help to:

Checklist

- ✓ break up your narrative (continuous writing)
- ✓ make your writing more lively
- ✓ make your characters more realistic and uncover more about their personalities.

Look at how part of the earlier, dull story about Ben can be changed into a livelier story by including dialogue.

> *Ben plodded home from school. "I'm so very tired," he muttered, "I need a rest."*
>
> *His mother greeted him as she heard him come in. "Hello, love, how was your day?"*
>
> *"Fine," Ben replied as he went upstairs. He got out his Lego and built a fantastic spaceship. "Mission control to Mr Spock. Can you hear me?" he made the astronaut say as he whizzed the spaceship through the air.*
>
> *"Ben! Tea!"*
>
> *"I'm coming." Ben ran downstairs and into the kitchen.*

In order to use dialogue, you must learn how to set out and punctuate speech.

Look again at the sections of dialogue in the story about Ben. What do you notice happens each time a different character speaks?

When writing dialogue you must remember to:

Checklist

- ✓ begin a new line or paragraph each time a different character starts to speak
- ✓ put speech marks before and after the direct speech
- ✓ finish a question with a question mark
- ✓ finish a statement with a full stop
- ✓ finish an order or an expression of surprise or excitement with an exclamation mark
- ✓ use commas, where needed, to separate **what** someone is saying from **who** said it or the **storyline**.

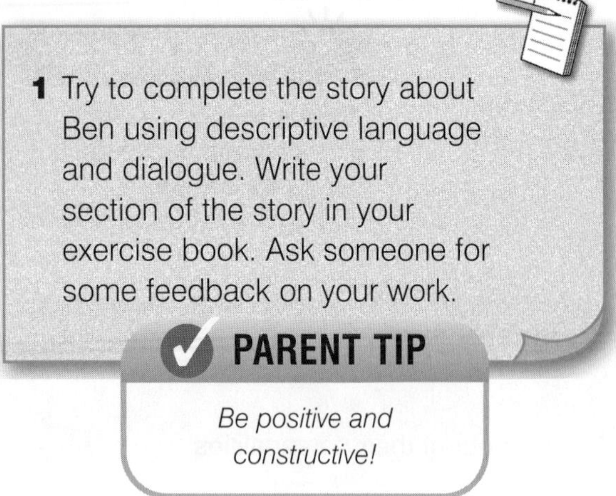

1 Try to complete the story about Ben using descriptive language and dialogue. Write your section of the story in your exercise book. Ask someone for some feedback on your work.

PARENT TIP

Be positive and constructive!

2 Look out for dialogue in your reading.

- See how authors use dialogue effectively.
- Look at how often they use it.
- Pay attention to how dialogue is punctuated. It can sometimes be rather complicated!
- Try to find ways of including dialogue in your own writing, if you don't already.

Add imagery

A way of adding more interest and detail to your writing is to include **imagery**. Imagery creates pictures in the reader's mind by comparing one thing with something different. The two most common types of imagery are **similes** and **metaphors**.

Most people find similes easier to spot and to use than metaphors. The word 'simile' starts like the word 'similar'. Similes compare one thing with another by using the word 'like' or the phrase 'as … as'.

Similes are a very effective way of describing something in a nutshell. For example:

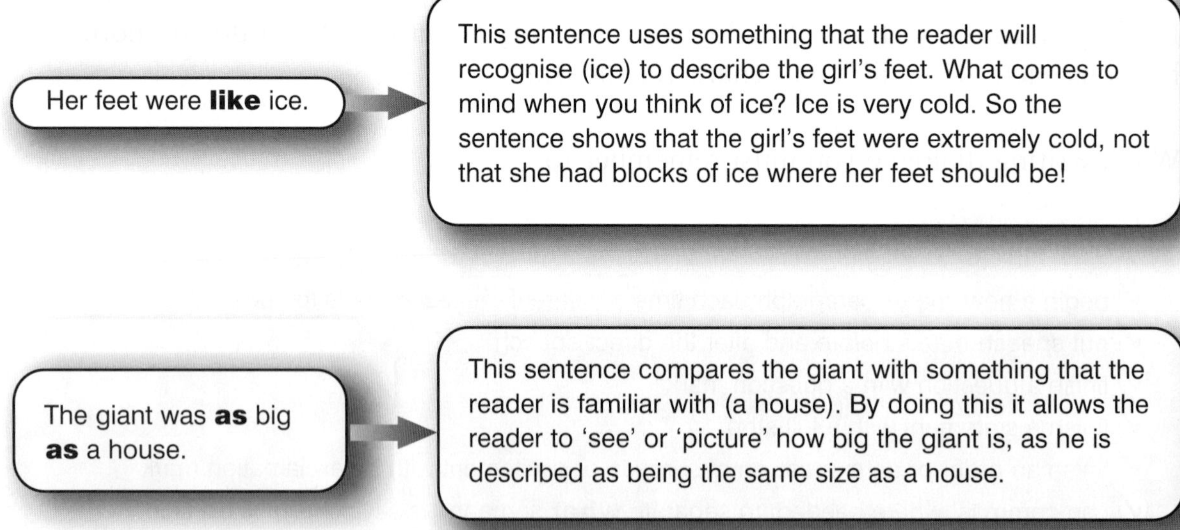

Her feet were **like** ice.
This sentence uses something that the reader will recognise (ice) to describe the girl's feet. What comes to mind when you think of ice? Ice is very cold. So the sentence shows that the girl's feet were extremely cold, not that she had blocks of ice where her feet should be!
The giant was **as** big **as** a house.
This sentence compares the giant with something that the reader is familiar with (a house). By doing this it allows the reader to 'see' or 'picture' how big the giant is, as he is described as being the same size as a house.

Many similes have been part of our language for centuries and it is important to know some of the most common ones. Here is a list of 15 of the most well-known ones:

as blind as a bat
as easy as pie
as fit as a fiddle
as dry as a bone
as tough as old boots

as busy as a bee
as brave as a lion
as clean as a whistle
as bold as brass
as white as snow

as deaf as a doorpost
as cool as a cucumber
as bright as a button
as quick as lightning
as sly as a fox

Some of the most common similes can be overused, so try to think up some new ones. A new simile can really surprise and amuse a reader. Here are some examples to get you thinking:

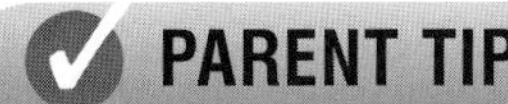

PARENT TIP

Children mostly absorb common similes, proverbs and idioms from hearing them at home. Use them whenever you can and explain their meanings.

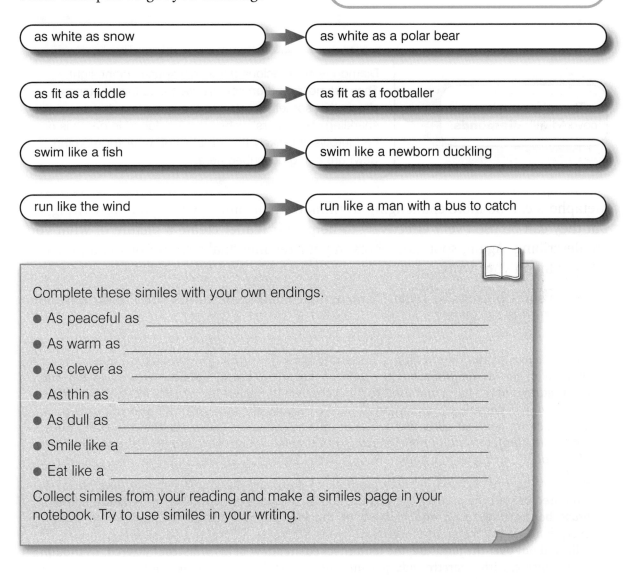

as white as snow → as white as a polar bear

as fit as a fiddle → as fit as a footballer

swim like a fish → swim like a newborn duckling

run like the wind → run like a man with a bus to catch

Complete these similes with your own endings.

- As peaceful as ________________
- As warm as ________________
- As clever as ________________
- As thin as ________________
- As dull as ________________
- Smile like a ________________
- Eat like a ________________

Collect similes from your reading and make a similes page in your notebook. Try to use similes in your writing.

Metaphors suggest similarities between two things but they do not make direct comparisons in the way that similes do. They describe something as if it were something else.

For instance, here are two simple sentences:

John lost his temper. The spider's web was covered with dew.

Look at how these sentences can be changed by using metaphors:

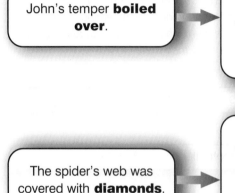

John's temper **boiled over**.

The phrase 'boiled over' is more commonly used to describe water that has reached its boiling point and is now frothing over the side of a saucepan, trying to push the lid up. This is the image which is created when we read the sentence about John. It shows that John is so angry that he is about to explode!

The spider's web was covered with **diamonds**.

Diamonds are precious gems that sparkle in the light. They are not found on spiders' webs, so this sentence shows that something else on the spider's web was sparkling. As spiders' webs are often found in gardens or hedgerows, it is likely that droplets of water (or morning dew) are being described here.

Metaphors can be more challenging to think of than similes when you are writing, but they can be used very effectively to help your reader create a picture of what you are describing. Again, spot metaphors in your reading, make collections and practise using some in your writing.

Here is a short passage by Dylan Thomas that includes several similes and metaphors. Can you find them all?

I was staying at the time with my uncle and his wife. Although she was my aunt, I never thought of her as anything but the wife of my uncle, partly because he was so big and trumpeting and red-hairy and used to fill every inch of the hot little house like an old buffalo squeezed into an airing cupboard, and partly because she was so small and silk and quick and made no noise at all as she whisked about on padded paws, dusting the china dogs, feeding the buffalo, setting the mousetraps that never caught her; and once she sneaked out of the room, to squeak in a nook or nibble in the hayloft, you forgot she had ever been there.

But there he was, always, a steaming hulk of an uncle, his braces straining like hawsers, crammed behind the counter of the tiny shop at the front of the house, and breathing like a brass band; or guzzling and blustery in the kitchen over his gutsy supper, too big for everything except the great black boats of his boots. As he ate, the house grew smaller; he billowed out over the furniture, the loud checked meadow of his waistcoat littered, as though after a picnic, with cigarette ends, peeling, cabbage stalks, birds' bones, gravy; and the forest fire of his hair crackled among the hooked hams from the ceiling.

From *A Story* by Dylan Thomas

Think about the senses

We discover everything around us through our five senses. We do this by:

seeing feeling hearing smelling tasting

So, what have these got to do with writing?

You can help your reader to really experience what you are writing about by using words that appeal to some or all of the five senses.

Most of what people write relates to what they **see** in their mind's **eye**. This encourages the reader to use their sense of **sight**.

Adding **dialogue** or describing **sounds** can introduce the sense of **hearing**.

By including other sense words in your descriptions, you can also appeal to the reader's sense of **touch**, **taste** and **smell**.

This table gives examples of five words for each sense. Copy it into your exercise book and see how many more sense words you can collect:

Sight	**Touch**	**Hearing**	**Smell**	**Taste**
blue	icy	clash	sickly	sour
shiny	scalding	patter	pungent	bitter
enormous	rough	boom	aromatic	spicy
glittering	smooth	soothing	fishy	delicious
cloudy	sticky	loudly	overpowering	sharp

In writing you can think of a **sixth sense**. You can feel with your sense of touch, using your fingertips, but you can also feel with your heart. (See the section: Think about feelings on page 32.) Describing characters' feelings can appeal to the reader's sense of **emotion**.

Here is a short passage describing summer, in which the author uses many of the senses. How many sense words or phrases can you find?

> *We sat by the roadside and scooped the dust with our hands and made little piles in the gutters. Then we slid through the grass and lay on our backs and just stared at the empty sky. There was nothing to do... Small heated winds blew over our faces, dandelion seeds floated by, burnt sap and roast nettles tingled our nostrils together with the dull rust smell of dry ground. The grass was June high ... the whole of it humming with blundering bees and flickering with scarlet butterflies.*
>
> From *Cider with Rosie* by Laurie Lee

Here are some activities which will help you think about your senses when you write:

- Try describing a place by using all of your senses.
- Choose an object from your room and write a description of it, without revealing exactly what the object is. Try to refer to all of your senses. Can someone else guess what it is?
- Write about an action like peeling an apple, running in a race or playing an instrument and refer to all of your senses.
- Shut your eyes and listen for a few minutes. Note down everything you heard.
- Close your eyes and feel the different textures of the objects around you. Can you think of words to describe what they feel like?
- Think about the four seasons and find sense words for each one.
- Collect powerful **onomatopoeic** words which can be used to imitate sounds, such as: **tick-tock splash twittering stomp crash** Comics are good places to find these!

PARENT TIP

Fun party games are: making 'feely' boxes or herb/spice packs to name; blindfold tasting sessions, etc.

Write clearly and legibly

Remember: if no one can read what you have written because it is not clear, is poorly spelt, badly punctuated, or doesn't make sense, then it's not worth writing! Take trouble over your handwriting. Learn to check (or proofread) so you can correct any mistakes and improve what you write.

It is useful to write in pencil when you are practising for 11+ English. This allows you to correct mistakes and make sure your writing can be easily read.

PARENT TIP

Make sure your child is sitting comfortably, holding his or her pencil in a relaxed way, and encourage him or her to use joined-up writing: it's quicker and looks more grown-up!

Remember:

Checklist

- ✓ whenever you write something, think about these **ten ways** of improving your writing
- ✓ which of these do you use already? Which do you forget to use?
- ✓ practise these ways as often as you can in your writing.

⑤ *Watch the time!*

"I'm hopeless at writing with a time limit."

You will always have a set amount of time to produce your writing in an 11+ English paper, because this is a test and to make a test fair, everyone has the same amount of time. It depends on who sets the test, but the whole exam is likely to last about one hour. You may only have half an hour to complete the writing task.

Many people, even if they enjoy writing at their own pace, find the thought of writing under timed conditions quite daunting. However, there are ways of helping you to use your time well.

Checklist

- ✓ Practise your writing skills whenever you can. You will be writing at school, but you also need to practise at home. During Years 5 and 6, before you do the 11+ exam, you will need to try writing under exam conditions.
- ✓ Make sure you know where the clock is before you start. This is important when you are practising, and in the exam itself.
- ✓ Before you start, check how long you will have for your writing test.
- ✓ Allow about five minutes to plan your writing.
- ✓ When you are about half way through your writing, have a quick look at the clock. This will help you to pace yourself for the second half.
- ✓ Leave about five minutes to check your writing.

Don't worry if you don't finish your writing in the time limit to begin with. Put a mark next to the point you had reached when the time ran out and then complete your writing. The mark will show you how far away you were from the end when the time was up.

If the time does run out before you finish, think about which sections took longest to write.

- Were all those details necessary?
- Could you have moved the story on faster and saved some time?

Thinking about these questions will help you learn how to pace yourself while you write.

It may be helpful to supervise the timing; it's tempting to keep on going once the time is up but this isn't possible in exams.

There will always be a time limit!

6 *Practise the skills!*

"How much do I need to write?"

It isn't easy to say exactly how much you should be able to write in a given time limit as:

- everyone's handwriting is different
- some people are very fluent and can write many pages in a short time
- some people prefer to plan and think first, so have less time to write
- some people get writer's block and can't think of very much to write

A useful guide is to try and write a page and a half in an exercise book in half an hour. This is a very rough guide, though. Always remember: it is **quality** not **quantity** that is most important.

Another useful guide is to aim to write one beginning paragraph, three or four middle paragraphs and an end paragraph (the conclusion). Again, this is a very rough guide to remind you of the **structure** of your writing. It depends what kind of writing you are doing.

REMEMBER!

Everyone can improve with practice, as long as they get feedback.

Here are some suggestions for story titles. Give yourself half an hour for each story. Try to find a quiet, well-lit, comfortable place to sit. Write in your exercise book.

Looking After a Pet for the Day
The Day the Queen Came to Tea
A Dream
A Family Outing
Why I Should Have Stayed in Bed
A Journey I Will Never Forget
A Day to Remember
A Change in Time
Secret Places
Seaside Holiday
The Deserted House
First Day at School
What a Disappointment!
Lost

REMEMBER!

1 Plan in paragraphs before you write.
2 Keep your ideas simple.
3 Remember the title.
4 Use a clear structure.
5 Develop your vocabulary.
6 Use full sentences.
7 Communicate clearly.
8 Entertain your reader.
9 Write legibly.
10 Watch the time.

PARENT TIP

Go over these aims whenever you are giving feedback. It can be quite hard for your child to stand back from his or her writing and be self-critical, so you have a vital part to play.

Ask someone to read your stories when you have finished each one and give you some feedback. If the comments are also written in your book below your writing, you will be able to read them before you write your next piece. They will be there as reminders and help to improve your story-writing skills.

For examples of children's writing, follow the Free Resources link at www.bond11plus.co.uk.

7 *Other kinds of writing*

Essays

An essay is a piece of writing where you are discussing a title. It could be a personal topic like 'My Friends', 'Pets I Know' or 'My Hobbies'. It could be something general like 'Hunting Foxes: For and Against' or 'The Advantages and Disadvantages of School Uniform'. This kind of essay can be called **persuasive writing** because you are trying to persuade your reader to agree with one point of view.

It may be useful to think of an essay title as being like a nut, which you need to crack open in your first paragraph. You need to show you understand what that title is about and what key words like 'Friends', 'Pets', 'Hobbies', 'Hunting' and 'School Uniform' mean.

Next it may be useful to put the title in the dock, as if in a trial. That way you can think of calling up your 'witnesses' to 'give evidence' and provide your opinions for and against the title. This can help give your writing a structure. A useful way to do this is to use phrases such as 'Firstly, secondly…' or 'On the one hand…. On the other hand…' to begin your paragraphs and make your points.

It is very important that you keep the title in mind all the time and not let yourself go off onto a different subject.

Towards the end imagine the judge summing up the evidence at a trial, drawing all the threads together and coming to a conclusion. This will be your final paragraph.

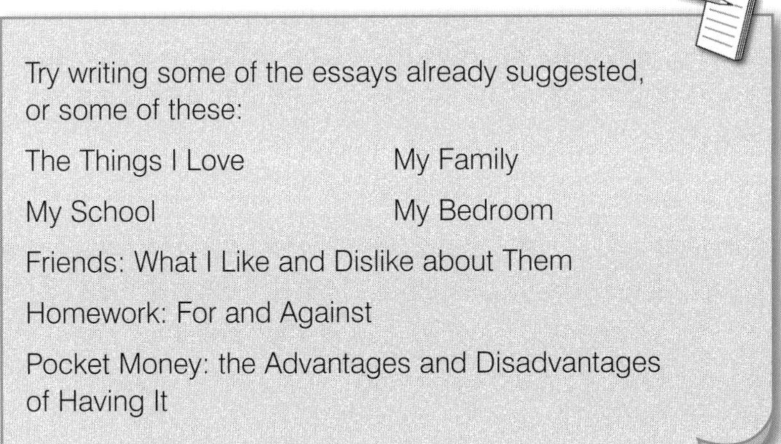

Try writing some of the essays already suggested, or some of these:

The Things I Love — My Family

My School — My Bedroom

Friends: What I Like and Dislike about Them

Homework: For and Against

Pocket Money: the Advantages and Disadvantages of Having It

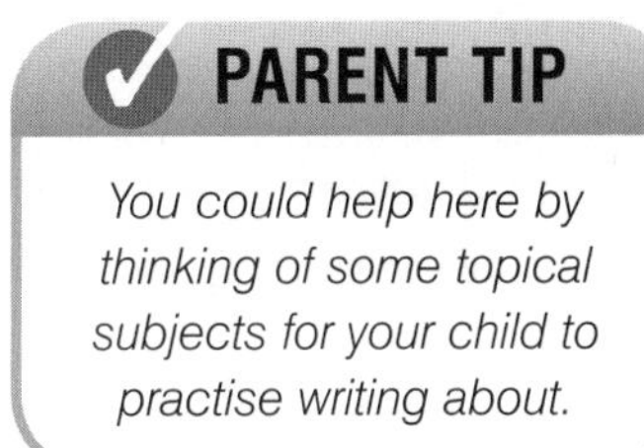

PARENT TIP

You could help here by thinking of some topical subjects for your child to practise writing about.

Letters

You may be asked to write a letter in 11+ English. This could be a **formal** or an **informal** letter. Remember, there are certain aspects that apply to all letters:

Checklist

- ✓ write the address and the date at the top of the letter on the right-hand side
- ✓ write in the first person, using 'I' or 'we'
- ✓ write in the present tense (usually).

Formal letters

Formal letters can be written for many reasons. You may be asking for information, complaining about something or explaining something. Whatever your reason for writing, all formal letters should follow a particular format:

Checklist

- ✓ put your name, address and the date clearly at the top of the letter on the right-hand side
- ✓ start with **'Dear'** and the person's name, or write **'Dear Sir/Madam'** if you don't know his or her name
- ✓ write in paragraphs:
  - in the first paragraph, explain why you are writing
  - in the middle paragraphs, add further details
  - in the final paragraph, draw the letter to a close and perhaps ask for a reply
- ✓ use formal words and be firm
- ✓ use a formal ending: **'Yours sincerely'** if you know the name of the person you are writing to; **'Yours faithfully'** if you don't.

Informal letters

An informal letter is one sent to family members, friends or penfriends for example. You can choose how to set it out and how you write it. If you are asked to write an informal letter in an exam, it is still important to write clearly and pay attention to sentences, spelling and punctuation.

Checklist

- ✓ You can start with 'Dear', but could choose other, more friendly, greetings: **'Hello'**, **'Hi'**. Follow this with the person's name.
- ✓ You could write in one paragraph.
- ✓ You could use informal words and a chatty tone.
- ✓ Finish with an informal ending: **'Love from...'**, **'Bye for now'**, **'Best wishes'**, **'Write soon'**.
- ✓ You may include a postscript **(PS)** to add something you forgot to mention in the letter.

Here are some ideas of the sorts of letters that you could be asked to write in 11+ English:

- Write to the Prime Minister explaining why children should have less homework.
- Write a letter to the town council arguing that your playing field should not be built on.
- Write a first letter to a new penfriend.
- Imagine you are on a week's adventure holiday. Write to a friend about your experiences.

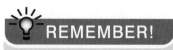

Before you start, work out whether the letter you have to write is formal or informal.

Find some letters at home and see how these are set out.

Having a penfriend is useful informal letter practice – and it's fun to receive letters back! Children's magazines often have penfriend pages.

Try writing some of the letter suggestions made above. Make up some of your own.

Recounts, reports and accounts

Recounts are used to 'retell' something. They can be personal, like a **report** about a school trip or a holiday, or impersonal like a newspaper article or an **account** of an historical event.

In your 11+ English paper, you could be asked to write a description of an event or an experience you have had. You could be asked to write a report of a school summer fair for the school magazine, or perhaps an account of your last holiday, trip abroad or a class outing.

When writing a recount, try to write as if you are telling the story of what happened. All recounts should be written in the past tense and they usually:

Checklist

- ✓ start with an introduction, explaining what the writing is going to be about
- ✓ are written in the first or third person (I/we or he/she/they)
- ✓ have an organised structure, written in paragraphs
- ✓ use time connectives: first, then, next, after, finally
- ✓ retell the events in the order they happened (chronological order)
- ✓ include technical terms if the topic needs them
- ✓ include details to make the retelling lively
- ✓ end with a closing sentence or paragraph that comments on the event or experience.

- Keep a diary with short accounts of special occasions.
- If your school has a magazine, try to write some reports of school events for it.
- Try writing a fictional account and a non-fiction report of the same event, such as 'The Day I Started School' or 'A Visit to the Dentist'.
- See if you can write a formal report and then an informal account of:

  a birthday party
  an important football, netball or rounders match
  a film
  a new place to visit

D Grammar and punctuation

"Those are the worst."

Both these parts of 11+ English tests can fill many children with alarm. What are they about?

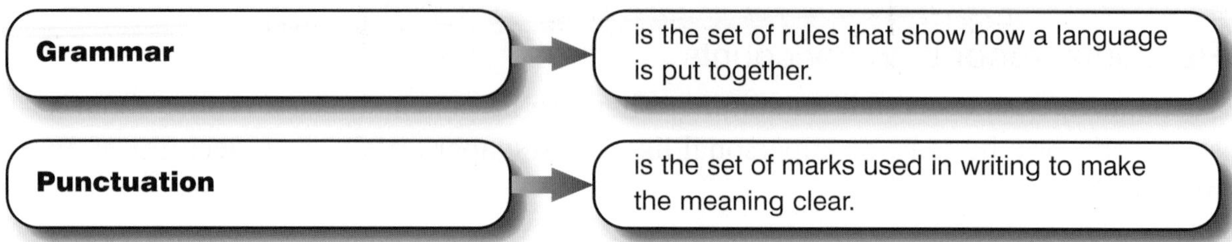

Grammar
is the set of rules that show how a language is put together.
Punctuation
is the set of marks used in writing to make the meaning clear.

You are already an expert on grammar. Amazingly, you learn to speak grammatically when you first start talking and then get better as you chat, watch TV, listen to stories and 'bathe' in your language.

If English is not your first language, then do plenty of 'bathing' in English! Immerse yourself in all aspects of it. Reading all sorts of different things and paying attention to what you read is the best way.

For 11+ English, you need to understand:

- sentences
- phrases and clauses
- paragraphs
- commas
- other common punctuation marks
- parts of speech
- subjects and objects
- gender and diminutives
- synonyms and antonyms
- abbreviations and acronyms
- compound words
- direct and reported speech

Each of these elements has a section of its own here. Read through any of the topics you need to brush up on and test your skills by doing the practice activities.

There is also a section on common grammar mistakes and what to do about them.

1 Sentences

"Whenever I take a big breath, I put a full stop."

This is quite a good way of starting to write in sentences. It will usually sound wrong if you take a large breath in the middle of a sentence. It can also be useful to check through your sentences in a piece of writing, noticing when you need to take a breath before carrying on. It is likely you will need to put a full stop in these places. In order to be sure, though, you need to know what a sentence is and what different kinds of sentences there are.

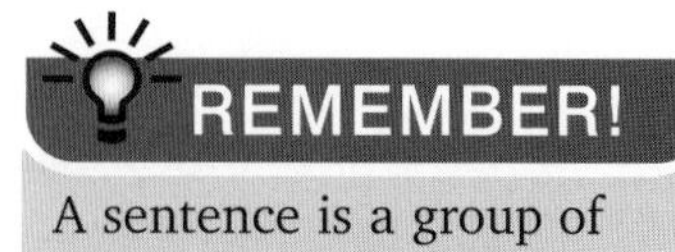

A sentence is a group of words that express a complete action or idea.

Practice Test

English 11+

Read the instructions carefully.

- Do not begin the test or open the booklet until told to do so.
- Work as quickly and as carefully as you can.
- Ring the correct letter from the options given to answer each question.
- You may do rough working on a separate sheet of paper.
- If you make a mistake cross out the mistake and write the new answer clearly.
- You will have 50 minutes to complete the test.

Published in 2006 by:
Nelson Thornes Ltd
Delta Place
27 Bath Road
CHELTENHAM
GL53 7TH
United Kingdom

06 07 08 09 10 / 10 9 8 7 6 5 4 3 2 1

A catalogue record for this book is available from the British Library

ISBN: 978 0 7487 9695 3

Page make-up by GreenGate Publishing Services, Tonbridge, Kent

Published by Nelson Thornes. Nelson Thornes is an Infinitas Learning company, and is not associated in any way with NFER-Nelson.

Read the extract carefully, then answer the questions.

'A Christmas Carol' by Charles Dickens tells the story of mean and lonely Mr Scrooge, who, on Christmas Eve, meets the ghosts of the past, present and future, who frighten him into changing his ways.

Once upon a time – of all the good days in the year, on Christmas Eve – old Scrooge sat busy in his counting house. It was cold, bleak, biting weather: foggy withal: and he could hear the people in the court outside, go wheezing up and down, beating their hands upon their breasts, and stamping their feet upon the pavement stones to warm them. The city clocks had only just gone three, but it was quite dark already – it had not been light all day – and candles were flaring in the windows of the neighbouring offices, like ruddy smears upon the palpable brown air. The fog came pouring in at every chink and keyhole, and was so dense without, that although the court was of the narrowest, the houses opposite were mere phantoms. To see the dingy cloud come drooping down, obscuring everything, one might have thought that Nature lived hard by, and was brewing on a large scale.

The door of Scrooge's counting house was open that he might keep his eye upon his clerk, who in a dismal little cell beyond, a sort of tank, was copying letters. Scrooge had a very small fire, but the clerk's fire was so very much smaller that it looked like one coal. But he couldn't replenish it, for Scrooge kept the coal-box in his own room; and so surely as the clerk came in with the shovel, the master predicted that it would be necessary for them to part. Wherefore the clerk put on his white comforter, and tried to warm himself at the candle; in which effort, not being a man of a strong imagination, he failed.

"A merry Christmas, uncle! God save you!" cried a cheerful voice. It was the voice of Scrooge's nephew, who came upon him so quickly that this was the first intimation he had of his approach.

"Bah!" said Scrooge, "Humbug!"

He had so heated himself with rapid walking in the fog and frost, this nephew of Scrooge's, that he was all in a glow; his face was ruddy and handsome; his eyes sparkled, and his breath smoked again. "Christmas a humbug, uncle!" said Scrooge's nephew. "You don't mean that, I am sure?"

"I do," said Scrooge. "Merry Christmas! What right have you to be merry? What reason have you to be merry? You're poor enough."

"Come, then," returned the nephew gaily. "What right have you to be dismal? What reason have you to be morose? You're rich enough."

Scrooge having no better answer ready on the spur of the moment, said "Bah!" again; and followed it up with "Humbug."

"Don't be cross, uncle!" said the nephew.

"What else can I be," returned the uncle, "when I live in such a world of fools as this? Merry Christmas! Out upon merry Christmas! What's Christmas time to you but a time for paying bills without money; a time for finding yourself a year older, but not an hour richer; a time for balancing your books and having every item in 'em through a round dozen of months presented dead against you? If I could work my will," said Scrooge indignantly, "every idiot who goes about with 'Merry Christmas' on his lips, should be boiled with his own pudding, and buried with a stake of holly through his heart. He should!"

"Uncle!" pleaded the nephew.

"Nephew!" returned the uncle sternly, "keep Christmas in your own way, and let me keep it in mine."

"Keep it!" repeated Scrooge's nephew. "But you don't keep it."

"Let me leave it alone, then," said Scrooge. "Much good may it do you! Much good it has ever done you!"

"There are many things from which I might have derived good, by which I have not profited, I dare say," returned the nephew. "Christmas among the rest. But I am sure I have always thought of Christmas time, when it has come round – apart from the veneration due to its sacred name and origin, if anything belonging to it can be apart from that – as a good time; a kind, forgiving, charitable, pleasant time: the only time I know of, in the long calendar of the year, when men and women seem by one consent to open their shut-up hearts freely, and to think of people below them as if they really were fellow-passengers to the grave, and not another race of creatures bound on other journeys. And therefore, uncle, though it has never put a scrap of gold or silver in my pocket, I believe that it has done me good, and will do me good; and I say, God bless it!"

The clerk in the Tank involuntarily applauded. Becoming immediately sensible of the impropriety, he poked the fire, and extinguished the last frail spark for ever.

"Let me hear another sound from you," said Scrooge, "and you'll keep your Christmas by losing your situation! You're quite a powerful speaker, sir," he added, turning to his nephew. "I wonder you don't go into Parliament."

"Don't be angry, uncle. Come! Dine with us tomorrow."

(Adapted from *A Christmas Carol* by Charles Dickens)

---

1 Which day does the story take place on? Circle the correct letter.

A New Year's Eve　**B** Boxing Day
C New Year's Day　**D** Christmas Day
E Christmas Eve

1

2 What was the weather like? Circle the correct letter.

A cold and rainy　**B** cold and sunny
C rainy and warm　**D** foggy and cold
E windy and warm

1

3 How do people outside try to keep warm? Circle the correct letter.

A They keep their hands in their pockets.　**B** They whistle to keep cheerful.
C They wear thick overcoats.　**D** They stamp their feet.
E They walk very quickly.

1

4 At what time of day does the story open? Circle the correct letter.

A before dawn　**B** at breakfast time
C mid morning　**D** afternoon
E night-time

1

5 What looked like phantoms in the fog? Circle the correct letter.

A the people passing by　**B** the light of the candles
C the horses and carriages　**D** the houses
E the church spires

1

6 Why did Scrooge have the door of his counting house open? Circle the correct letter.

A to watch the people in the street　**B** to watch his clerk
C to see if his nephew was coming　**D** to let some air into the room
E to talk to his clerk

1

6 TOTAL

7 What was the clerk's main job? Circle the correct letter.

A copying letters
B keeping the fire going
C answering the telephone
D guarding the office
E helping customers

1

8 Why did the clerk have such a small fire? Circle the correct letter.

A He was too busy working.
B He was quite warm enough.
C There was no more coal.
D Scrooge would not let him have any more coal.
E He was going home soon.

1

9 What did the clerk use to try to keep warm?

1 a white scarf   2 thick boots   3 a candle   4 a fire   5 a hat

Circle the correct letter.

A 1 and 2
B 3, 4 and 5
C 2 and 4
D 3
E 1, 3 and 4

1

10 What word best describes Scrooge's nephew when he comes in? Circle the correct letter.

A angry
B sad
C cold
D excited
E miserable

1

11 What does the word 'morose' mean (line 29)? Circle the correct letter.

A unkind
B generous
C miserable
D ill
E old

1

12 Why does Scrooge think people are fools to call Christmas a merry time? Circle the correct letter.

A because they are richer and wiser
B because presents don't make them happy
C because they are older and poorer
D because it is over very quickly
E because the weather is always so cold

1

13 How do you cook a Christmas pudding? Circle the correct letter.

A You bake it.
B You boil it.
C You fry it.
D You grill it.
E You steam it.

1

7 TOTAL

14 What does Scrooge think that his nephew finds himself doing at Christmas? Circle the correct letter.

A eating and drinking a lot
B giving presents
C going away on holiday
D paying bills and settling his accounts
E seeing his friends

1

15 Why does Scrooge's nephew like Christmas? Circle the correct letter.

A It makes him richer.
B It is cold and sunny.
C He gets time off work.
D People are kind to each other.
E He comes to see his uncle.

1

16 The clerk is described as 'not being a man of a strong imagination' (line 16). What does this mean here? Circle the correct letter.

A He is not strong.
B He is not very clever.
C He is unhealthy.
D He is mad.
E He is old.

1

17 What happened when the clerk poked the fire? Circle the correct letter.

A It burned brighter.
B It warmed the room more.
C Nothing.
D The flames got smaller.
E It went out.

1

18 Scrooge said to his clerk, "…you'll keep your Christmas by losing your situation." (line 58). What does he mean? Circle the correct letter.

A You will have Christmas Day off because you will lose your job.
B You will have to work on Christmas Day and lose your pay.
C Your Christmas will be a very miserable one.
D You will have a good Christmas because you will be warm.
E On Christmas Day I will remove your chair.

1

19 What type of work does Scrooge suggest to his nephew? Circle the right letter.

A clerk
B Member of Parliament
C doctor
D soldier
E lawyer

1

20 Which word best sums up Scrooge's personality? Circle the correct letter.

A foolish
B cheerful
C brave
D mean
E sensible

1

21 What is the most important thing in Scrooge's life? Circle the correct letter.

A being unkind to his clerk
B seeing his nephew
C making money
D keeping warm
E helping people

1

8 TOTAL

22 What is Scrooge's general view of people? Circle the correct letter.

A They are fools.
B They are poor.
C They are unpleasant.
D They are kind.
E They are lazy.

1

Answer the following questions about these words and phrases.

23 Which word in this sentence is an adjective? Circle the correct letter.

"Don't be cross, uncle!" said the nephew.

A Don't
B be
C cross
D uncle
E said
F the
G nephew

1

24 What parts of speech are '**Nature**' (line 9) and '**stake**' (line 39)? Circle the correct letter.

A adverbs
B nouns
C prepositions
D adjectives
E verbs

1

25 Which of these words is a preposition? Circle the correct letter.

A open (line 11)
B kept (line 14)
C imagination (line 17)
D upon (line 19)
E quickly (line 19)

1

In this extract there are a number of spelling mistakes. Circle the letter where the spelling mistake is underlined or, if there isn't a spelling mistake, circle the letter X.

26 He caught sight of the house (**A**) beyond, but, when he drew nearer, (**B**) it disappeared (**C**)

sudenly (**D**) behind the neighbouring hedge. **X**

1

27 A feeling of incredible anger, (**A**) as he waited hopelessly outside, (**B**) began to grow (**C**)

silently within him. (**D**) **X**

1

28 The door swung noisily open, (**A**) without any human presence visible. (**B**)

Nervously he started forward, (**C**) hopeing that the owner (**D**) would appear. (**E**) **X**

1

7 TOTAL

29 "Boy!" called an agetated voice. Henry jumped, frightened by the sudden sound
A B C

echoing in the empty hall.
D X | 1

30 A wizened, ancient man, clothed all in a black gown, was standing silently,
A B C

hiden by obscuring shadows.
D X | 1

31 A scrawny hand clutched his. It was cold as marbel. He could see a beaked nose
A B C

and peering weasel's eyes.
D X | 1

32 He tried impatiently to pull away, but the grip silently tightened.
A B

An imense feeling of dread started to invade his body.
C D X | 1

33 He stared hard, trying to imagine how he might escape those aweful eyes.
A B C D X | 1

In this extract mistakes have been made in the use of punctuation and capital letters. Circle the letter where the mistake is or, if there isn't a mistake, circle the letter X.

34 Emma hurtled outside and shouted, "Help, Uncle Sam, help! Peter's injured"
A B C D X | 1

35 I'd hardly been in a house with a pool before, though wed rented one once.
A B C D X | 1

36 The walls were lovely and light with windows in the roof.
A B

A door at the end led outside I hoped that it went into the garden.
C D X | 1

37 It was a french book, which she couldn't read, though she hoped with luck
A B C

that her uncle could translate it.
D X | 1

38 "Theres no hope, I'm afraid. The money's been stolen. We'll not see it again."
A B C D X 1

39 The enormous sack, weighted, with gold, was impossible to lift. It wouldn't budge.
A B C D X 1

40 "What's the worry" he asked. "You'll be there by nightfall if you don't lose the
A B C

path, or stop."
D X 1

41 The monkeys looked puzzled at the way the bananas were growing and some
A B C

even thought it was a trick.
D X 1

42 He waited thinking it would be dark soon. Then he'd leave, completely unseen.
A B C D X 1

In this extract, the letter below the best word or words needs to be chosen so the extract makes sense and uses correct English. Circle the correct letter.

43 He waited, silently hoping the beast couldn't wouldn't shouldn't could've return.
A B C D 1

44 The beast growled. There wasn't the best most hopeful greatest faintest hope
A B C D

of rescue. 1

45 He hoped that the branch would beer bear bare bring his weight.
A B C D 1

46 There was a loud crack. He hurried howled hurtled skipped to the ground.
A B C D 1

47 He ran slowly slyly kindly nervously towards the safety of the hill.
A B C D 1

48 He had almost completely utterly totally made it, when disaster struck.
A B C D 1

49 The beast, roars roaring roared roar loudly, stood over him.
A B C D 1

50 Its giant paw stealthily heavily slowly lightly came down on his head.
A B C D 1

50 TOTAL

Here are some useful checklists about sentences:

A sentence:

Checklist

- ✓ starts with a **capital letter**
- ✓ must contain a **verb** (see page 59)
- ✓ usually contains a **subject** (see page 63)
- ✓ ends with a **full stop, question mark or exclamation mark**
- ✓ is **complete**.

There are many different kinds of sentences. Here are some of the main ones:

- a **statement**: He got out of bed.
- a **question**: Is he out of bed yet?
- an **order** or **command**: "Get out of bed!"
- an **exclamation**: "You're already out of bed!"

Question marks (?) and exclamation marks (!) are special types of punctuation marks that can end sentences.

You need to be aware that a sentence can be:

Checklist

- ✓ **short:** two or three words, e.g. Josh wailed.
- ✓ **long:** often these are shorter sentences joined together with connectives, e.g. Josh wailed **because** he had fallen down and cut his knee.

Good writing will usually have a mixture of different sentence lengths.

You also need to recognise that a sentence can be:

Checklist

- ✓ **simple:** made up of only one clause (see page 51), e.g. Josie played the recorder.
- ✓ **complex:** made up of more than one clause or phrase (see page 51), e.g. Josie played the recorder in the concert, while Anish accompanied her on the piano and the choir sang.
- ✓ **active:** someone or something is doing something, e.g. Josie played her recorder in the concert.
- ✓ **passive:** something is being done to someone or something, e.g. The recorder was played by Josie in the concert.

Notice where sentences start and stop and look out for all of these sentence types in your reading.

"I can spot sentences when I read but I forget about punctuation when I'm writing."

This happens because you are telling yourself what you want to write in your head first, and we don't put punctuation marks in our thoughts. What we say flows from sentence to sentence. The punctuation is not obvious and sentences merge into one another. You can tell when sentences stop and start from their sound, though. There are separate things you want to say, and each separate thing is a sentence. Listen to people talking and see where you think the full stops should go. By becoming aware of sentences as you read, you can also check your own writing for sentences. All it takes is practice!

REMEMBER!

If you are able to write down in sentences what you make up in your head, then the chances are that your **grammar** will be correct.

REMEMBER!

If your sentences have capital letters at the beginning and full stops, question marks or exclamation marks at the end, then you are already coping with the most important aspect of **punctuation**.

Can you sort out the sentences in this passage? There are eight capital letters and eight full stops missing.

but they were not listening, none of them were they were staring out over the sea, a look of utter astonishment on every face there was nothing there but the sound at first, a curious roaring and crying from the open sea beyond Popplestones that became a crescendo of snorting and whistling within minutes Popplestones was alive with whales great spouts of water shot into the air everywhere you looked in the bay shining black backs broke the surface, rocked a little and then rolled forward and vanished again under the water all of Big Tim's friends had already fled up the beach, but he stayed with us, mesmerised as we were beside us, the stranded whale writhed and rolled in its grave of sand, its tail thrashing in fury and frustration, its own whistling cry joining the chorus of the others out in Popplestones

Adapted from *Why the Whales Came* by Michael Morpurgo

PARENT TIP

Point out incorrect sentences you come across to your child. It is amusing for him or her to see that adults find correct sentence structure hard to grasp too!

② *Phrases and clauses*

"I'm not sure what the difference is between these two."

Many people don't find it that easy to tell the difference between phrases and clauses. These checklists and examples should help to make the differences clear.

A **phrase** is a group of words that:

Checklist

- ✓ makes **sense**
- ✓ does **not** contain both a subject and a verb
- ✓ is **not** complete.

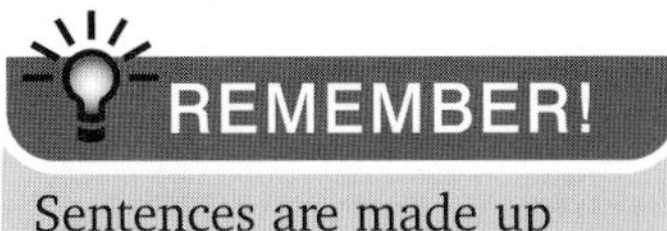

Sentences are made up of phrases and clauses.

You need to be able to recognise phrases as being part of a sentence.

Here are some examples:

the long way home   under his coat   over the moon

A **clause** is a group of words that:

Checklist

- ✓ **contains** a subject and a verb
- ✓ is **complete**.

There are two types of clause: a **main** clause and a **subordinate** clause.

A **main** clause:

Checklist

- ✓ makes sense **on its own** as a complete sentence.

Here are some main clauses using the phrases above:

we went the long way home   he'd hidden it under his coat
she was over the moon

A **subordinate** clause:

Checklist

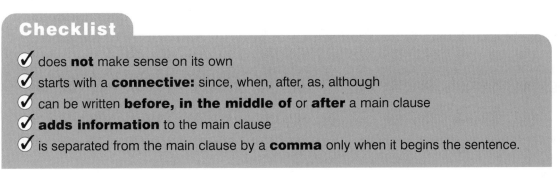

- ✓ does **not** make sense on its own
- ✓ starts with a **connective:** since, when, after, as, although
- ✓ can be written **before, in the middle of** or **after** a main clause
- ✓ **adds information** to the main clause
- ✓ is separated from the main clause by a **comma** only when it begins the sentence.

If you put main and subordinate clauses together, you can make complex sentences.

Here are the main clauses from above, with examples of subordinate clauses attached:

After the concert, we went the long way home.

He'd hidden it under his coat when Reuben wasn't looking.

Although she had school the next day, she was over the moon.

You need to be able to recognise main and subordinate clauses and use them in your writing.

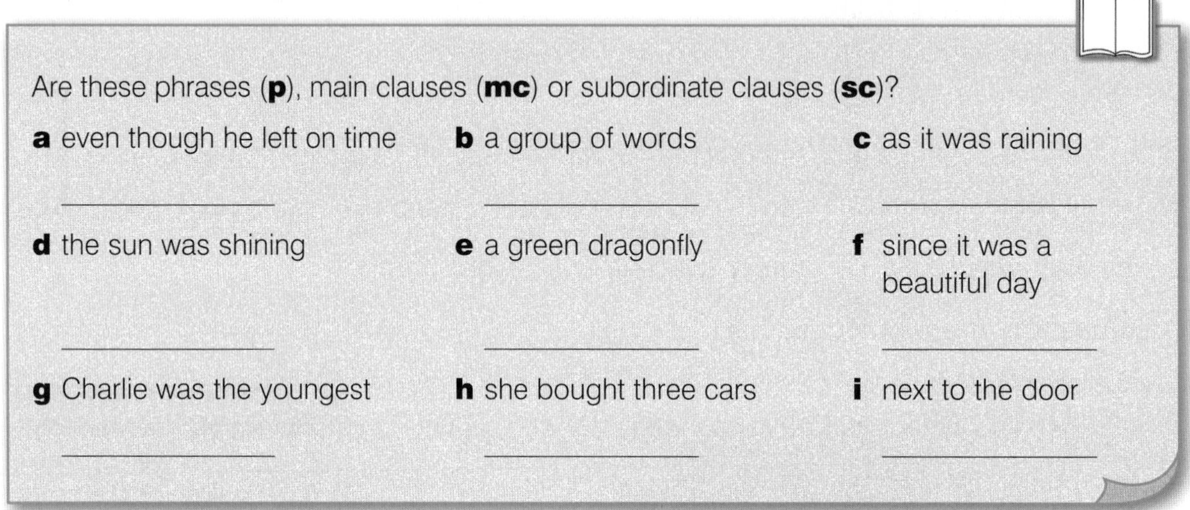

Are these phrases (**p**), main clauses (**mc**) or subordinate clauses (**sc**)?

a even though he left on time ____________

b a group of words ____________

c as it was raining ____________

d the sun was shining ____________

e a green dragonfly ____________

f since it was a beautiful day ____________

g Charlie was the youngest ____________

h she bought three cars ____________

i next to the door ____________

Now look at how these short sentences can be transformed by adding phrases or clauses.

Jim was swimming. The water was freezing. He dived. His head grazed the bottom.

A You could join them all together with **connectives** to make one long sentence:

Jim was swimming and the water was freezing so he dived but his head grazed the bottom.

B You could add **phrases** to extend the shorter sentences:

Jim, dressed in shorts, was swimming. The water in the crystal blue pool was freezing. Taking a deep breath, he dived, dragging himself to even colder water. All of a sudden, his head grazed the bottom.

C You could add **clauses** to the short sentences by using **connectives** or **conjunctions**:

Jim was swimming while his dad was fishing. Although the sun was shining, the water was freezing. He took a deep breath and dived. Even though the pool was deep, his head grazed the bottom.

Study sentences carefully as you read. Notice how phrases and clauses are used and practise using them correctly in your own writing.

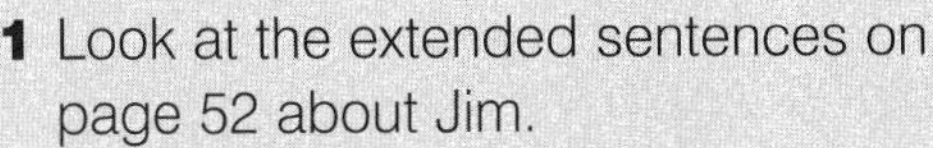

1 Look at the extended sentences on page 52 about Jim.

- Underline the connectives in A.
- Underline the phrases in B.
- Underline the main clauses in C.
- Put brackets round the subordinate clauses in C.
- Circle the connectives that start the subordinate clauses in C.

2 Here are four short sentences:

A dragonfly skimmed by. It settled. Its wings quivered. Another joined it.

- Join them into one longer sentence.
- Extend each sentence by adding phrases.
- Add clauses to each sentence.

Which do you prefer?

3 *Paragraphs*

"Paragraphs are four or five lines of writing in a story."

Some teachers may encourage you to write in paragraphs following rules like this. However, if you look at paragraphs in books, you will see that they are all different lengths. There is no limit to the number of paragraphs a piece of writing can have.

Paragraphs are a form of punctuation. They show how sentences are grouped together. Using paragraphs makes your writing easier to read because they break up a piece of writing into sections or stages.

A new paragraph:

Checklist

- ✓ starts on a new line
- ✓ is often **indented** (a space between the margin and the first word) or, if the first line is not indented, a **line space** is left between paragraphs
- ✓ shows a change in subject or aspect: a new place, time or person
- ✓ is used in writing dialogue, each time a different character starts talking.

A paragraph is a group of sentences or 'chunk' of text that describes one stage in a piece of writing.

Look out for how and when paragraphs are used in your reading. Practise using them in your own writing. (See Planning, page 21.)

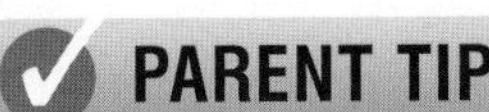

Point out how you can spot paragraphs by looking for indented lines or where each block of text is separated by a line space. Ask your child to tell you the first and last words in a paragraph. You can take it in turns to read aloud, paragraph by paragraph, which can soon make paragraphs clearer.

4 Commas

"When I take a breath, I put a comma."

Many children put full stops when they take a breath, too. This means it can be a tricky way of working out when to put commas or full stops.

There are a variety of reasons for using commas in sentences.

Commas are used to:

Never end a sentence with a comma!

Checklist

- ✓ **separate clauses** in a sentence, e.g.

  Jim sat quietly**,** as he had been chosen to direct the play**,** and watched his friends go through it.
- ✓ **separate items** in a short list, e.g.

  There were crisps**,** biscuit crumbs**,** empty wrappers and sticky glasses on the table in front of him.
- ✓ **separate dialogue** (talking) from narrative (the storyline), e.g.

  "We keep forgetting our words**,**" giggled Sandy and Alan.

  "Come on**,**" Jim said**,** "you're not really trying."
- ✓ **separate terms of address** from the rest of the sentence, e.g.

  A little later he called, "Sandy**,** that was much better. Hey**,** everyone**,** how about practising that again?"

You can see how important commas are in making the meaning of sentences clear, by reading these sentences without commas:

> Jim sat quietly as he had been chosen to direct the play and watched his friends go through it. There were crisps biscuit crumbs empty wrappers and sticky glasses on the table in front of him.
>
> "We keep forgetting our words" giggled Sandy and Alan.
>
> "Come on" Jim said "you're not really trying."
>
> A little later he called "Sandy that was much better. Hey everyone how about practising that again?"

You can see that commas have much more important jobs than simply saying, "Take a breath now". Certainly, when you feel the need to take a breath, there should probably be some kind of punctuation, but not necessarily a comma.

There are 15 commas missing from this continuation of the above story. Can you find where they need to go?

The children rehearsed their play several times finding that it was becoming a smoother more successful performance. Jim pleased with the progress they were making decided to call for a break. "Let's grab a bite from the kitchen" he suggested "and then if you like we can go out for some fresh air exercise and a change of scene."

The others agreed and Alan suddenly remembering he had promised to phone his mother made a quick phone call. "It's going really well Mum" he said. "Tell Dad Giles Uncle Bob and Ellie to be ready for six o'clock."

5 *Other common punctuation marks*

"I often forget to put question marks."

"I put exclamation marks all over the place."

"I don't understand how to use all the other marks."

Apart from full stops and commas, there are a number of other common punctuation marks. Here they are:

! ? ... ; : ' " " - – ( )

Some of them are found at the end of sentences; others are written inside sentences. How many do you use already? Read the summary of any punctuation marks you're not sure how or when to use.

Finishing sentences

You know that full stops finish sentences (statements). There are three other forms of punctuation that can finish a sentence:

! **Exclamation marks** help to show emphasis or emotion (such as excitement, surprise or anger). They are used to finish:

Checklist

✓ an **order** or **command:** Stop**!** Wait**!** Be careful**!**

✓ an **exclamation:** That was amazing**!** Goodness**!** It was too much**!**

REMEMBER!

Be sparing and only use one ! at a time. Otherwise your writing can become very 'over the top'.

? **Question marks** finish:

Checklist

✓ **a sentence that asks a question:** Can you help**?** What's his name**?**

An **ellipsis** allows a sentence to trail off and creates suspense, so this mark finishes:

Checklist

- ✓ **any sentence that leaves the reader guessing:** It didn't take her long to notice**...**

Inside sentences

You have seen how commas have different roles in sentences. There are several other types of punctuation mark which each have their own job. You need to be able to recognise these marks and use them in your writing.

Semicolons show longer pauses in sentences. They are used:

Checklist

- ✓ **instead of commas in long or complex lists:**
  Lee went off to fetch two parasols**;** a jug of iced water**;** a set of playing cards**;** towels for lying on and ice creams all round.
- ✓ **to link two or more related sentences instead of full stops or conjunctions:**
  It was hot**;** the sun was beating down**;** we were all bathed in sweat.

Colons introduce different elements such as:

Checklist

✓ **a list:**	The recipe needed**:** two eggs; 250 g flour; a pinch of salt; 500 ml milk.
✓ **an explanation:**	I have two pet hates**:** spiders and mosquitoes.
✓ **a quotation:**	The note said**:** "Come at 2 p.m. Bring your bike."

Apostrophes have two very different jobs. They:

Checklist

✓ **replace missing letters in contractions:**	we would = we**'**d; he cannot = he can**'**t
✓ **show belonging (possession):**	the fur belonging to the cat = the cat**'**s fur the room belonging to Sushi = Sushi**'**s room the bikes belonging to the boys = the boys**'** bikes

Remember: **'it's'** always means either **'it is'** or **'it has'**. Don't add an apostrophe to **'its'** to show possession.

Never use apostrophes to make plurals! (See page 82.)
Look closely at where you put an apostrophe for singular or plural nouns.

There are many examples of apostrophes being used incorrectly. Spotting these with your child can be fun and it can be instructive to discuss how to correct them.

“ ” **Speech marks** are used when dialogue is written. They come:

Checklist

- ✓ **before and after the words that are actually spoken:**
  "Come here," called Akshay, "and I'll tell you the secret."

\- **Hyphens** have two main jobs. They:

Checklist

- ✓ **join two or more words together to make a new idea:**
  father-in-law part-time self-confidence sixty-three non-stick
- ✓ **split a word at the end of a syllable if the whole word will not fit on one line:**
  It was late and Ella noticed that the air was grow-
  ing cooler.

– **Dashes** can be used alone or in pairs.

A single dash:

Checklist

- ✓ **attaches an extra point to a sentence:**
  He thought it was his cat under the bed – but was it?

Dashes are often used in informal writing and in dialogue.

A pair of dashes:

Checklist

✓ **separates non-essential information from the rest of a sentence:**
Our first house **–** the one in the town centre **–** had a small garden.

( ) **Brackets** always come in pairs. They are used to:

Checklist

✓ **insert useful (but not essential) details in a sentence, like dashes:**
Our first house **(**the one in the town centre**)** had a small garden.

✓ **separate numbers and abbreviations from the rest of a sentence:**
His flight **(**no. LHR 7604**)** went from London Heathrow airport **(**LHR**)**.

Look out for all kinds of punctuation in your reading and ask yourself, whenever you see a punctuation mark, what it is for. Practise using the punctuation you see in your own writing. Especially look out for how speech is punctuated and the use of speech marks, commas and paragraphs.

From your reading, make collections of the following in your exercise book:

- ten sentences that finish with exclamation marks, question marks or ellipses
- ten sentences that show the different uses for semicolons, colons, dashes and brackets
- ten examples of both hyphen uses
- ten examples of both uses of apostrophes, including the whole sentence each time.

Look out for all these different types of punctuation in your reading and try to use them in your writing.

6 *Parts of speech*

"It's quite tricky to work out parts of speech."

Yes, it can be!

Words are divided into different groups depending on their use. In 11+ English you must show that you know the main groups. These are:

- nouns
- verbs
- adjectives
- adverbs
- pronouns
- prepositions
- connectives (or conjunctions)

First, you need to learn the different job each group does in English grammar. A brief summary of each of these word groups is given in this section. Read through any that you need to brush up on and complete the practice activities to check what you know.

Nouns

- **Common** nouns are **general names** of people, places, feelings, things and events. For example:

people:	crowd	teacher	police officer
places:	school	garden	supermarket
feelings:	fear	happiness	curiosity
things:	balloon	air	computer
events:	party	holiday	sports day

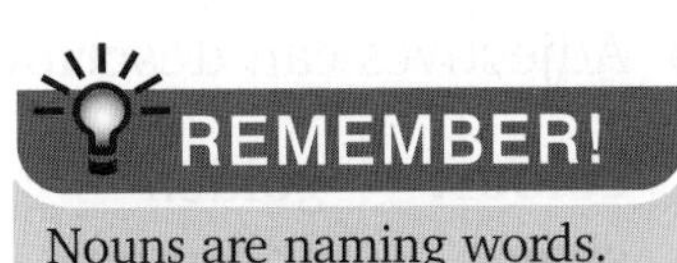

REMEMBER!

Nouns are naming words.

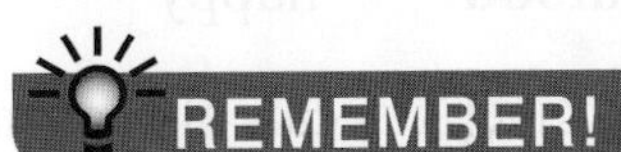

REMEMBER!

Most common nouns can be singular or plural. Some nouns are always plural: **scissors.**

- **Proper** nouns are **special names** (or titles) of people, places, things or events. For example:

people:	Tom	Mum	Mr Scott
places:	Birmingham	Spain	Derbyshire
things:	July	Playstation	Woolworths
events:	Christmas	Yom Kippur	Diwali

REMEMBER!

All proper nouns start with capital letters.

- **Abstract** nouns are names of a **concept** or an **idea**. For example:

beauty love appearance vacancy leadership

- **Collective** nouns are names of a **group** or **collection** of things. For example:

flock of sheep board of directors swarm of bees bunch of flowers

Verbs

- Verbs can be:

doing words:	jump	swim	read
being words:	like	know	am

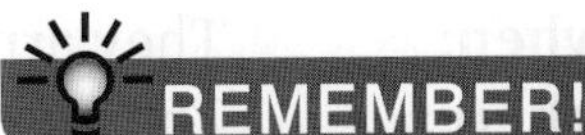

REMEMBER!

Verbs are **action** words. They tell you what is happening to the subject or noun in a sentence.

REMEMBER!

The name of a verb is called the **infinitive**. It always has 'to' in front:
to do to jump to swim to read to like to know to be

- The **tense** of a verb tells you **when** something is happening:

present:	**I go** to the shops.	or	**I am going** to the shops.
past:	**I went** to the shops and **I bought** some bread.		
future:	**I will go** to the shops and **I will buy** some bread.		

- Verbs must **agree** with the singular or plural subject of a sentence. (See Section 7.)

  I am hungry. **You are** hungry. **He is** hungry. **They are** hungry.

- The verbs **'to have'** and **'to be'** are special verbs called **auxiliary** verbs. They are sometimes called 'helpers' and are used with other verbs in sentences:

  I **am** going home. We **have** lost our cat. Our neighbours **are** looking for it.

Adjectives

- Adjectives can **describe**:

colour:	golden	green	transparent
size:	enormous	medium	tiny
mood:	happy	miserable	uncertain

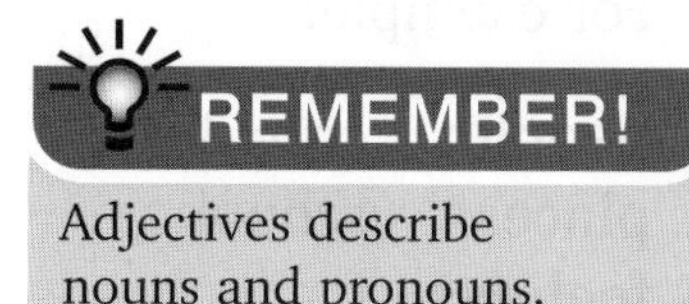

Adjectives describe nouns and pronouns.

- Adjectives can also **compare** things. There are three groups of comparing adjectives:

simple:	A hedgehog is small.	(No ending is added to the adjective.)
comparative:	A mouse is smaller.	('-er' is added to the adjective.)
superlative:	An ant is the smallest.	('-est' is added to the adjective.)

  These endings are usually added to adjectives with **one syllable** or adjectives with **two syllables that end in '-y'**. The words '**more**' or '**most**' are written before adjectives with **two or more** syllables instead of these endings, e.g.

  This book is **more** helpful. This is the **most** popular book.

Adverbs

- Adverbs describe **how, when, where** and **how often** something happens:

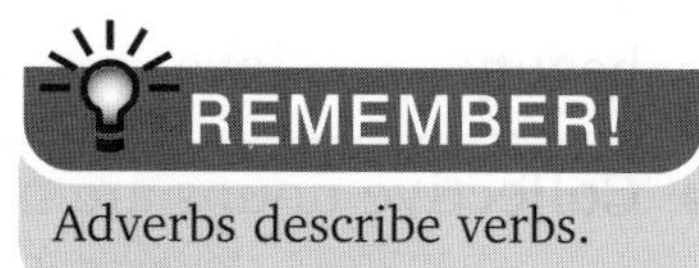

Adverbs describe verbs.

how:	He ran **slowly**.	She read **quietly**.
when:	They arrived **early**.	The shop opened **late**.
where:	The boys played football **outside**.	She walked **upstairs**.
how often:	I practise my trumpet **regularly**.	You **often** go to visit her.

Pronouns

There are two groups of pronouns that replace common and proper nouns in particular ways.

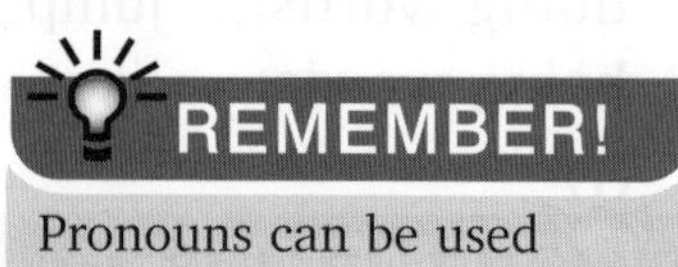

Pronouns can be used instead of nouns.

- **Personal** pronouns can be singular or plural:

Jackie left for school at 7.30 a.m.	= **She** left for school at 7.30 a.m.
Paul and **Amruta** worked on **the project** together.	= **They** worked on **it** together.
Ted and I went to see **Matthew** and **Evie**.	= **We** went to see **them.**
Has **Danny** seen the **film**?	= Has **he** seen **it**?

- **Possessive** pronouns tell us who or what owns or has something:

That bike belongs to **Kang**.	= That bike is **his**. or It's **his**.
This book belongs to **me**.	= This is **my** book. or This book is **mine**.
The new car belongs to **Jo and Kim**.	= The new car is **theirs**. or It's **theirs**.
The house belongs to **us**.	= This is **our** house. or The house is **ours**.
The cat has a new, red collar.	= **Its** new collar is red.

There are two other kinds of pronouns that are often used in sentences:

- **Relative** pronouns are used to join two parts of a sentence. There are different relative pronouns to refer to different things.

who	refers to **people**:	This is Marise **who** lives next door.
which	refers to **things**:	I like this book **which** I read most evenings.
that	refers to **people and things**:	Here is a model **that** Jack built.
		He's the boy **that** lives next door.

- **Indefinite** pronouns refer generally to people or things:

Tell me all that you know.	= Tell me **everything**.
Tell me a thing you know.	= Tell me **something**.
Tell me one thing or other you know.	= Tell me **anything**. or Tell me **nothing**.
Show me all the people there.	= Show me **everyone**.
Show me one person there.	= Show me **someone**.
Show me one person or another there.	= Show me **anyone**. or Show me **no one**.

Prepositions

'Pre-' means 'before' or 'in front of'. A **pre**position is written in front of a noun.

- Prepositions **link** nouns and pronouns to other parts of a sentence. They show:

position:	**in** the room	**behind** the house	**near** the school
direction:	**up** the stairs	**through** the window	**over** the fence
time:	**during** break	**before** assembly	**on** Saturday

Connectives (or conjunctions)

Connectives can be:

short words:	if	but	then	so	while
compound words:	however	meanwhile	therefore	nevertheless	whereas
short phrases:	because of	as a result	due to	on the other hand	

(See Section 11, page 68, for more details on compound words.)

REMEMBER!

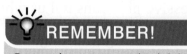

Connectives **connect** (or join) clauses or sentences together to make more complex sentences.

Once you understand these main parts of speech, you need to be able to spot them in your reading and use them in your writing. Try the exercises in the box below for practice:

Read this short passage:

James put the diary down and looked around him, feeling slightly dazed. It was something of a shock to see his room quite normal and ordinary, football boots hanging from the hook behind the door, pyjamas protruding from under the pillow, books, pictures, all in the proper place. No green and white wallpaper, no Aunt Fanny chattering on breathlessly, no Arnold watching with sparkling eyes as the Rector intoned his stern words for the dismissal of Thomas Kempe...

From *The Ghost of Thomas Kempe* by Penelope Lively

Using a red pen:

1. underline five proper nouns
2. put brackets round eight adjectives
3. put circles around four pronouns

Using a blue pen:

1. underline 15 common nouns
2. put brackets around three adverbs
3. put circles around six prepositions

- highlight 11 verbs
- draw boxes around two connectives

PARENT TIP

Raise your child's awareness of different kinds of words and how they can be used to improve sentences. Make use of these terms yourself to reinforce them in your child's mind. A useful exercise is to set a timer for five minutes and see how many of a particular part of speech (e.g. nouns) your child can highlight in that time in a page from a newspaper. Go over the ones he or she has found and discuss any errors.

7 Subjects and objects

"These words sound the same to me!"

Yes, many people find them a little confusing. Working through this section should help to make them clearer.

Most complete statements and questions have a subject and a verb. Orders and exclamations often leave out one or both of these.

The **subject** of a sentence is usually a common or proper noun or a noun phrase (a group of words including a noun). Remember:

Checklist

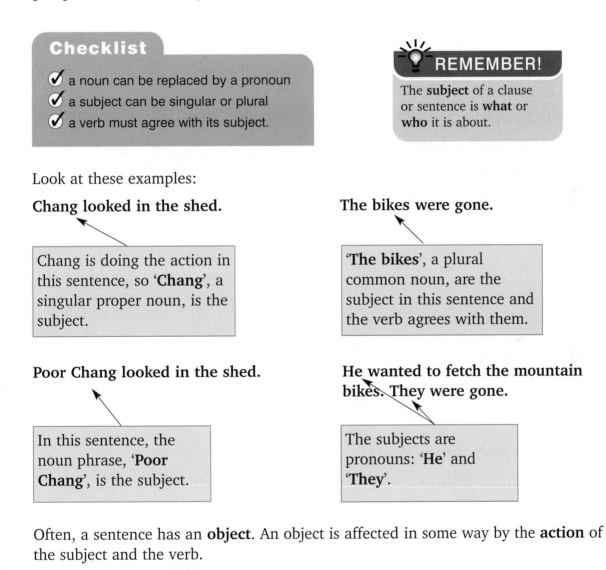

- ✓ a noun can be replaced by a pronoun
- ✓ a subject can be singular or plural
- ✓ a verb must agree with its subject.

The **subject** of a clause or sentence is **what** or **who** it is about.

Look at these examples:

Chang looked in the shed.

Chang is doing the action in this sentence, so '**Chang**', a singular proper noun, is the subject.

The bikes were gone.

'**The bikes**', a plural common noun, are the subject in this sentence and the verb agrees with them.

Poor Chang looked in the shed.

In this sentence, the noun phrase, '**Poor Chang**', is the subject.

He wanted to fetch the mountain bikes. They were gone.

The subjects are pronouns: '**He**' and '**They**'.

Often, a sentence has an **object**. An object is affected in some way by the **action** of the subject and the verb.

Look again at this sentence:

Chang looked in the shed.

'Chang' is the subject.

'looked' is the verb.

'the shed' is the object affected by the subject and the verb.

Look at this sentence:

He wanted to fetch the bikes.

'He' is the subject.

'wanted to fetch' is the verb.

'the bikes' is the object.

1 For each of these sentences, underline the subject or subjects in red, the object in blue and circle the verb. Then change the subjects and objects to pronouns and write the new sentences on the lines.

a The bird hopped among the branches. ______________________________

b Susie and I collected conkers. ______________________________

c The hockey players won the competition. ______________________________

2 Add objects to these sentences.

a The boy climbed ______________________________

b Our dog likes eating ______________________________

c None of the children wanted to bring ______________________________

3 Write a subject and a verb for each of the objects to complete the sentences.

a ______________________________ under the hedge.

b ______________________________ some flowers in the meadow.

c ______________________________ ten sums on the board.

8 *Gender and diminutives*

"I find these words quite hard to remember."

They can look rather off-putting! But they will come in very useful once you understand them.

In 11+ English you may need to show that you know the **gender** of nouns: whether they are **masculine** or **feminine**.

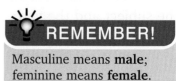

Masculine means **male**; feminine means **female**.

Many nouns have different words for male and female nouns. Sometimes the suffix '-ess' is added to a male word to make the female version. Look at the examples below.

Masculine	Feminine	Masculine	Feminine
hero	heroine	father	mother
prince	princess	count	countess
lord	lady	goose	gander
nephew	niece	stag	doe

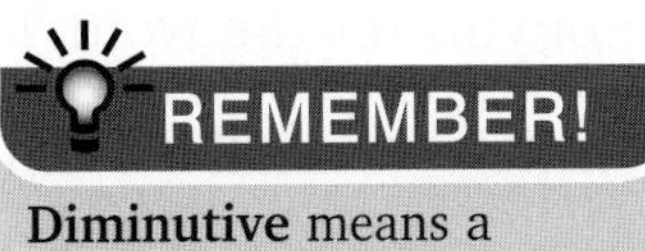

Diminutive means a **smaller** version of something.

You also need to know the **diminutive** forms of some nouns for 11+ English. In the case of animals, diminutives mean their babies or young. In the case of objects, diminutives mean **smaller versions** of them.

Some diminutives are formed by adding a **prefix** or a **suffix** to a root word. (See page 88.) Look at the examples below.

Larger form	Diminutive form	Larger form	Diminutive form
bus	minibus	goose	gosling
book	booklet	pig	piglet
kitchen	kitchenette	computer	microcomputer

Diminutives can be used as **nicknames** for first names. For instance, Nicholas is often shortened to Nick. Here are some more examples:

Full first name	Diminutive form	Full first name	Diminutive form
Christina	Chris	Matthew	Matt
Victor	Vic	Rajesh	Raj
Elisabeth	Liz	Rebecca	Becky

Make a collection in your exercise book of as many words as you can find where the masculine noun is different from the feminine noun. This particularly applies to jobs, animals and family members. If you can, add the diminutive forms as well.

Here are some to get you started:

duck fox waiter cow uncle host bride pig bachelor

9 Synonyms and antonyms

"I get a bit muddled with these."

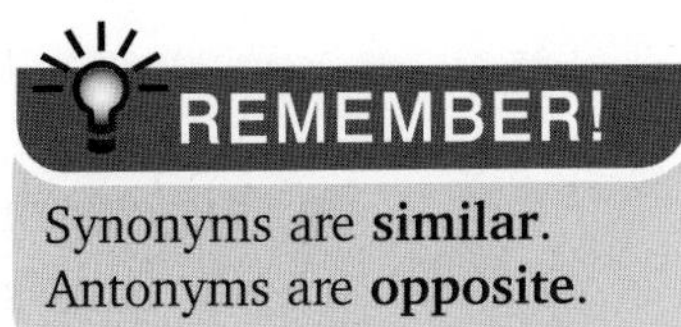

Synonyms are **similar**. Antonyms are **opposite**.

You may need to show that you know what these words mean in 11+ English.

Synonyms are words which have the same or similar meanings. For instance, here are some synonyms for the word 'large':

grand big sizeable huge bulky significant substantial

Using synonyms in your writing helps to avoid repetition and can make your writing more interesting. (See page 34 for more details on synonyms.)

Antonyms are words which have opposite meanings. For instance, here are some antonyms for the word 'large':

little small minute tiny skinny insignificant miniature

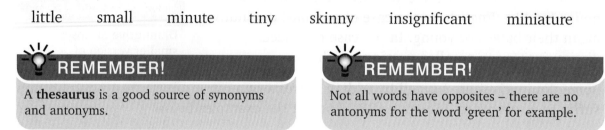

A **thesaurus** is a good source of synonyms and antonyms.

Not all words have opposites – there are no antonyms for the word 'green' for example.

Always think about meanings before using synonyms and antonyms. In English, we have many words with dozens of different meanings. If you look up words like 'mark' or 'catch' or 'play' in a dictionary, you will find numbers showing several versions of the same word and explaining the different meanings.

The words you choose must always fit the **context** (meaning) of a sentence. You may also need to think about parts of speech. (See page 58.)

Look at these examples:

The parcel felt very **light**.

There are many synonyms for the word 'light'. For example:

glow; weightless; insubstantial; ignite; delicate; soft; pale; elegant; bright.

All of these have different meanings and you need to understand the context of the sentence before choosing a synonym. In this example, 'light' means 'not heavy', so '**insubstantial**' would be a good synonym to use here.

The colour of my walls is **light** blue.

There are also many antonyms for the word 'light'. For example:

dark; gloomy; shade; heavy; serious; sinister; extinguish.

You can't choose the most appropriate antonym if you haven't understood the meaning of 'light' in the sentence. In this sentence, 'light' means 'pale', so '**dark**' would be a suitable antonym.

I switched on the **light**.

In this example, the word 'light' is a **noun**, not an **adjective**. This means suitable synonyms would be '**lamp**', '**torch**' or '**lantern**'. For this meaning, 'light' has no antonym.

Find synonyms and antonyms for these words:

timid sorry cross white cautious danger smooth courage single good

Remember: there could be different meanings and different alternatives! How many can you find?

10 *Abbreviations and acronyms*

"There are hundreds!"

Yes there are but no one expects you to know them all! Many individual words and groups of words are often shortened when used in speech or writing. You should make sure you are familiar with some of the most common abbreviations and that you can recognise some useful acronyms.

Here are some common abbreviations, which use part of the original word:

Abbreviation	**Full word**
bike	bicycle
fridge	refrigerator
photo	photograph
phone	telephone
rhino	rhinoceros

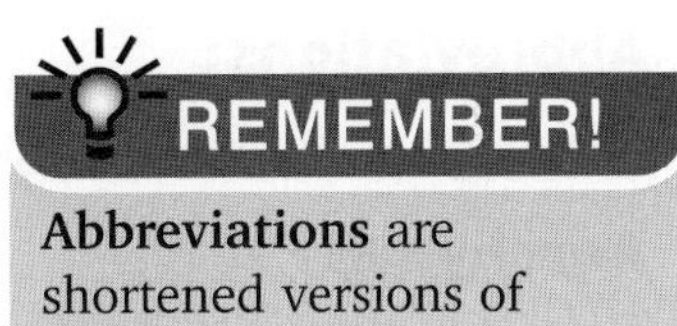

Did you know that all of the words in the left-hand column were abbreviations?

Abbreviations can also be formed from the first letters (initials) of the words being shortened. For example:

Abbreviation	**Full phrase**
BBC	**B**ritish **B**roadcasting **C**orporation
CD	**c**ompact **d**isc
HGV	**h**eavy **g**oods **v**ehicle
PC	**p**ersonal **c**omputer or **P**olice **C**onstable
RSPB	**R**oyal **S**ociety for the **P**rotection of **B**irds

Some other commonly used abbreviations come from Latin. For these you will need to understand what the phrase means rather than learn the Latin words they stand for. The examples below are often used in writing:

Abbreviation	**Full meaning**
a.m.	before noon
e.g.	for example
etc.	and so on
PS	written afterwards
v.	against

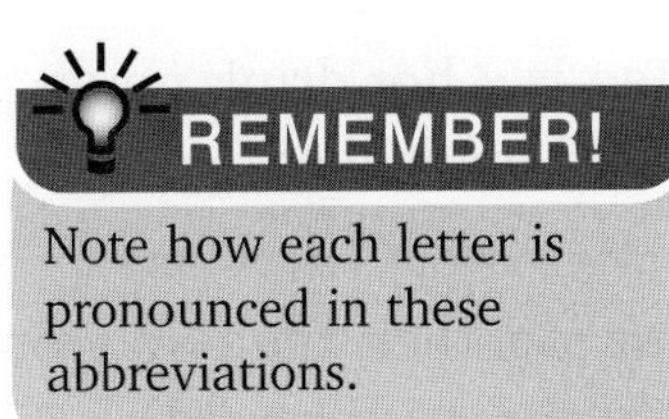

REMEMBER!
Note how each letter is pronounced in these abbreviations.

An acronym is a form of abbreviation which is usually made up of the initial letters of the group of words being shortened. Acronyms are different to the abbreviations listed in the second table above, as they are pronounced as single words.

Here are some acronyms you may recognise:

Acronym	Full phrase
FIFA	**F**édération **I**nternationale de **F**ootball **A**ssociation
laser	**l**ight **a**mplification by **s**timulated **e**mission of **r**adiation
NATO	**N**orth **At**lantic **T**reaty **O**rganisation
Ofsted	**Of**fice for **St**andards in **Ed**ucation
RAM	**r**andom-**a**ccess **m**emory

Did you know what these acronyms stood for?

Collect as many abbreviations and acronyms as you can in your exercise book and learn what they stand for. Here are some to start you off:

Abbreviations:

HQ GMT bus RSPCA PTO

Acronyms:

ASBO Ofcom ASH INSET

Listen for how often abbreviations and acronyms are used in speech and think about them when writing dialogue.

11 Compound words

"I'm not quite sure what they are."

Many people find compound words puzzling!

Compound words are made by joining two or three smaller words together to make a longer one.

Here are two examples of compound words:

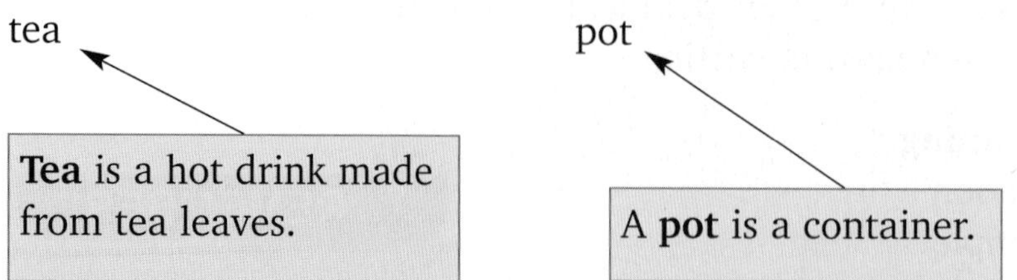

tea
pot
Tea is a hot drink made from tea leaves.
A pot is a container.

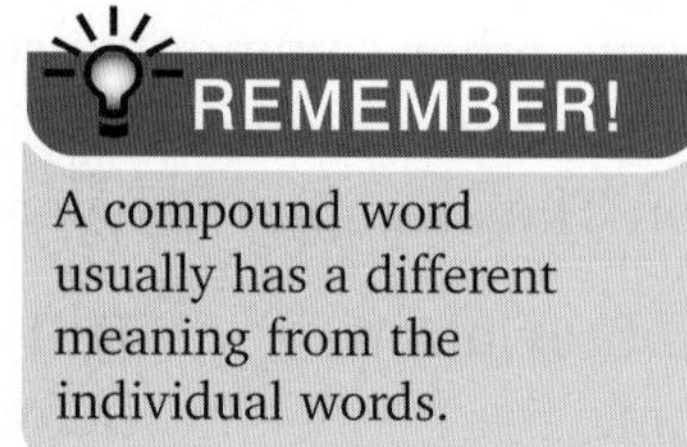

REMEMBER!
A compound word usually has a different meaning from the individual words.

Put together, the two words make a new idea: **teapot** (a covered pot with a spout in which tea is brewed).

work

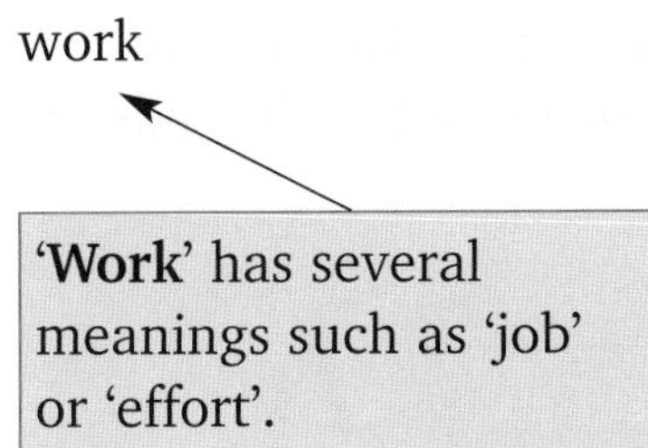

'**Work**' has several meanings such as 'job' or 'effort'.

man

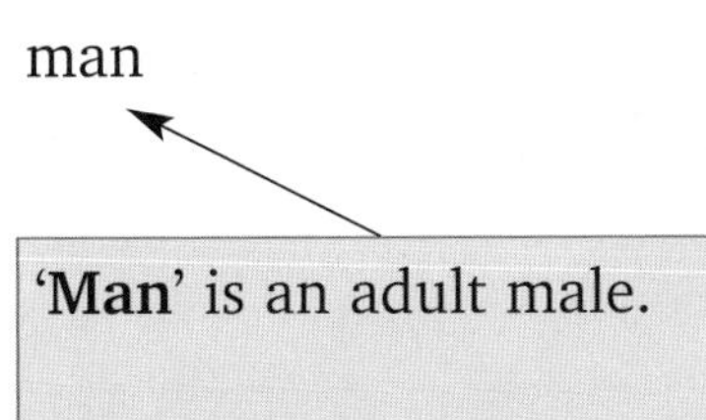

'**Man**' is an adult male.

ship

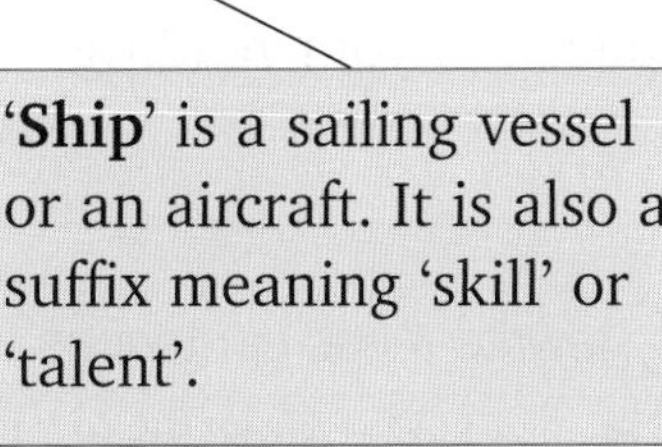

'**Ship**' is a sailing vessel or an aircraft. It is also a suffix meaning 'skill' or 'talent'.

Put together, the three words make a new idea: **workmanship** (the talent of a skilled manual worker).

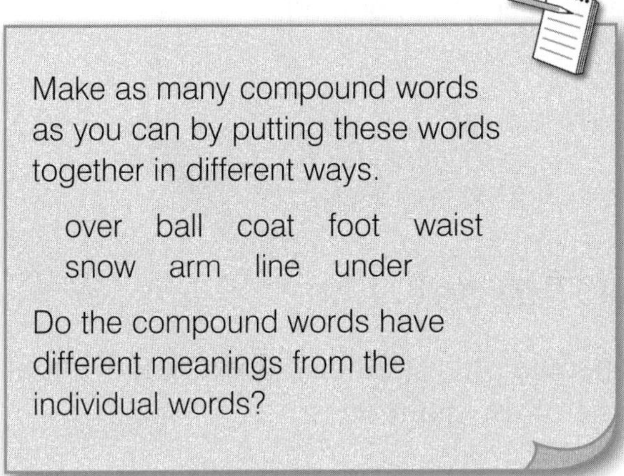

Make as many compound words as you can by putting these words together in different ways.
over ball coat foot waist
snow arm line under
Do the compound words have different meanings from the individual words?

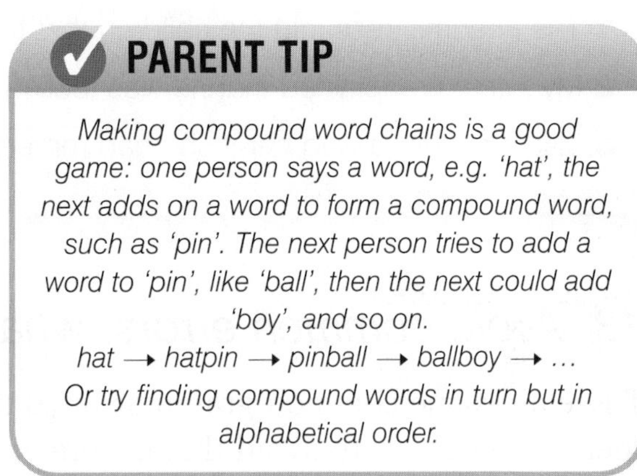

PARENT TIP
Making compound word chains is a good game: one person says a word, e.g. 'hat', the next adds on a word to form a compound word, such as 'pin'. The next person tries to add a word to 'pin', like 'ball', then the next could add 'boy', and so on.
hat → hatpin → pinball → ballboy → ...
Or try finding compound words in turn but in alphabetical order.

12 *Direct and reported speech*

"I find changing from one to the other tricky."

It can be quite tricky; there is a lot to think about!

There are two ways of writing speech which you need to be familiar with.

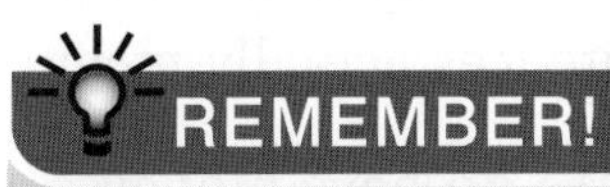

When writing direct speech, remember to pay close attention to all the punctuation needed.

- **Direct speech:**

  uses the words that are actually spoken, for instance:

  Jarek called, **"Help me! I'm drowning!"**

- **Reported speech:**

  explains what was said but does not use the exact words. You can write the same thing as if you are reporting something. So, in reported speech, the above example could be written as:

  Jarek called for help because he thought he was drowning.

Notice especially how the **tense** changes between direct and reported speech. In the first example, Jarek's words are written in the **present** tense. When his words are written as reported speech, the sentence is written in the **past** tense. This is quite tricky and you need to practise changing one to the other. Look out for both kinds of speech in your reading.

Rewrite these sentences as reported speech in your exercise book.

1 "I'd like a party for my birthday, Mum," said Dan.

2 Mr Slater remarked, "It feels like winter today."

3 "Come inside, Charlie," invited the old man, "and have a cup of tea with us."

Now change these reported speech sentences to direct speech.

1 The headmistress told the children that their behaviour was improving.

2 My father complained that he was feeling tired.

3 Lisa's mother asked her if she had remembered the note.

13 *Avoid common errors: what NOT to do!*

There are some common grammar traps that people often fall into. If you know about them, you can try to avoid them. Here are some of the main ones:

Double negatives

If you use two negative words in a phrase or sentence, these are called double negatives. Here are some examples:

We **don't** have no money.

There **weren't no** sweets left in the jar.

If you really think about them, the two negatives cancel each other out, so the sentences actually mean:

We **do** have money.

There **were** sweets left in the jar.

To avoid this problem you have to use the words '**any**' or '**no**'. For instance, the first example of double negatives could be correctly written as:

We don't have **any** money. or We have **no** money.

How should the second example be written?

When you are writing dialogue, though, it can be amusing to use double negatives now and again; people often use them when they're talking. Listen out for examples of this or find examples in dialogue in your reading.

'Of' or 'have'?

We should **have** gone, since they could **have** taken us.

In the sentence above, notice the use of '**have**'. This is a **conditional** sentence, based on what might have happened if…

When you say the sentence aloud, you will notice that the word 'have' gets swallowed up and sounds more like '**of**'. You must never write 'of' if you want to use correct grammar.

If you want to 'swallow' the 'have' to make it sound more like 'of', then use **contractions** in your writing. Using contractions, the example above would be written:

We should'**ve** gone, since they could'**ve** taken us.

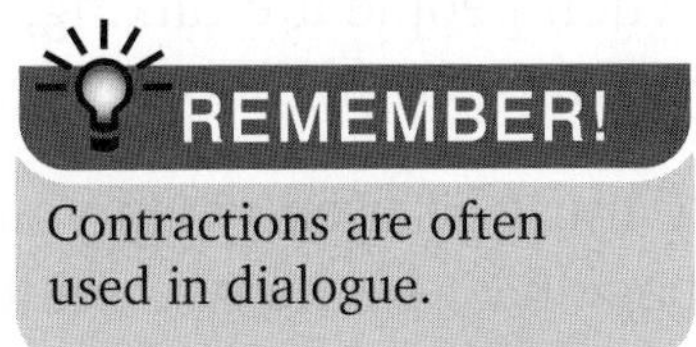
REMEMBER!
Contractions are often used in dialogue.

How often do you write 'of' instead of 'have'? Look out for this error in your own writing!

Past tenses

These can cause problems because there are many irregular forms that do not follow familiar patterns. Listen to a three-year-old talking and you will hear some mistakes that crop up in older children's writing too!

"I hurted my knee and it bleeded so I did cry."

The three-year-old has not yet learnt to say:

"I **hurt** my knee and it **bled** so I **cried**."

You need to learn irregular past tenses as you come across them. Here are some common irregular tenses that you should be familiar with:

Infinitive	**Present tense**	**Past tense**
to buy	I buy	I bought
to catch	you catch	you caught
to eat	he eats	he ate
to keep	she keeps	she kept
to make	it makes	it made
to run	we run	we ran
to speak	they speak	they spoke
to swim	they swim	they swam

Sometimes, when English is spoken, people will use different forms of the past tense. There is nothing wrong with these, but there are **standard forms** that you should know for 11+ English.

For instance, many people will say:

"I **done** my homework last night."

You need to know that in **Standard English** the correct way to say and write this is:

"I **did** my homework last night."

'I' or 'me'?

Many people find deciding on whether to use '**I**' or '**me**' in a piece of writing challenging.

Look at these examples of children's writing:

Me and my brother went out to play football.

Su Lin and me handed in our homework on time.

When people are talking, they often make mistakes in these kinds of sentences. When you are writing, however, you need to show that you know whether to use 'I' or 'me'.

'I' must be used when you are the **subject** or one of the subjects of the sentence. (See page 63.) In the two sentences above, it would be clearly wrong to say:

"Me went out to play football." or "Me handed in my homework on time." because you are the subject. If you are doing something with someone else, then the other person's name comes first. That's only polite!

The correct versions of these two sentences should be:

My brother and I went out to play football.

Su Lin and I handed in our homework on time.

My aunt sent it to you and I.

Dad told Pete and I to wait for him.

'Me' must be used when you are the **object** of the sentence. If you split the sentences up into two, it makes it easier to see what is happening.

My aunt sent it to you. My aunt sent it to **me**.

Dad told Pete to wait for him. Dad told **me** to wait for him.

The correct versions of these two sentences should be:

My aunt sent it to **you and me**.

Dad told **Pete and me** to wait for him.

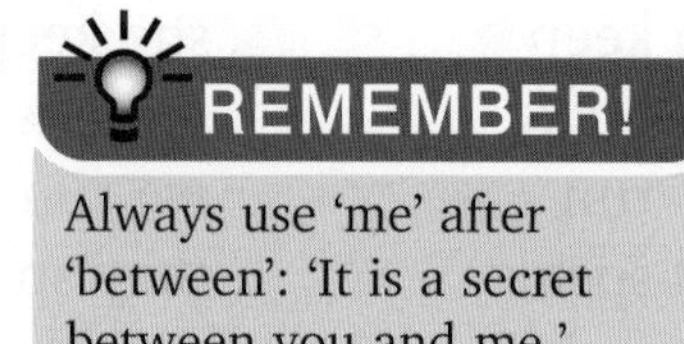

Always use 'me' after 'between': 'It is a secret between you and me.'

'Better' or 'best', 'worse' or 'worst', 'fewer' or 'less'?

These forms of adjectives can cause many people problems. You have to make sure that you use the correct form of the adjective when you are comparing.

These sentences are wrong: This jacket is the best of the two.

Sula is the worse chatterbox in the class.

Annie made less mistakes than Rob.

These sentences are correct: This jacket is **the better of** the two.

You are comparing two jackets, so that is why you need the comparative form 'better' rather than 'best'.

Sula is the **worst** chatterbox in the class.

You need to use the **superlative** form, not the **comparative** form for describing Sula because there are more than two people in her class.

Annie made **fewer** mistakes than Rob.

Use 'less' for amounts of something but 'fewer' for numbers of things, e.g.

There's **less** water in your bottle than in Lucy's.

There are **fewer** bottles in the fridge today than there were yesterday.

(See page 60 for more details on how to form comparative adjectives.)

Look out for these adjective uses in your reading and try to use them correctly.

14 *Practise the skills!*

1. Here is a punctuation test. This paragraph has been written without any punctuation. The following punctuation marks are in the right order. Put each punctuation mark in the right place. You will have to add some capital letters, too.

, , , ? . , , . , , .

how can i describe a vision of those rocks and those trees standing upright in those waters their bases dark and sinister their tops tinted by shades of red intensified by the pure reflection of the water we were scaling rocks that crumbled and let loose stones that crashed down behind us with the muffled rumble of an avalanche to the right and the left were caves and grottos hollowed out in the rocks gloomy and impenetrable to the eyes elsewhere there were vast clearings which seemed to have been created by human hands and i wondered whether i might not suddenly come face-to-face with some inhabitant of these waters

Adapted from *Twenty Thousand Leagues Under the Sea* by Jules Verne

2. Try to sort out this dialogue from *Alice in Wonderland*, setting it out into paragraphs for each new speaker, by putting a mark (/) each time there should be a new line. Write it correctly in your exercise book.

"Have some wine," the March Hare said in an encouraging tone. Alice looked all round the table, but there was nothing on it but tea. "I don't see any wine," she remarked. "There isn't any," said the March Hare. "Then it wasn't very civil of you to offer it," said Alice angrily. "It wasn't very civil of you to sit down without being invited," said the March Hare. "I didn't know it was your table," said Alice; "it's laid for a great many more than three." "Your hair wants cutting," said the Hatter. He had been looking at Alice for some time with great curiosity, and this was his first speech. "You should learn not to make personal remarks," Alice said with some severity. "It's very rude."

Adapted from *Alice's Adventures in Wonderland* by Lewis Carroll

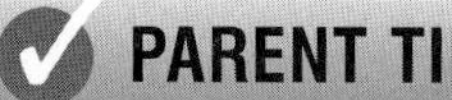

PARENT TIP

For further practice in grammar and punctuation, work through the range of activities in the Bond Assessment Papers in English *and* Bond 11+ Test Papers in English.

E Spelling

In 11+ English you need to show that your spelling is as accurate as you can make it. It is important that you are careful and try to spell so that what you have to say can be understood by someone else.

The English language can be quite challenging to spell. Some people seem to be very good at it. They tend to be wide and attentive readers who are interested in words. Many people struggle. The words just won't stick.

"I'm awful at spelling."

Before you work through this section, you could try the dictation test found in the Free Resources section for this book at www.bond11plus.co.uk to see how good you are at spelling already. Many of the words in the test are examples of the types of words with which children often have problems. Ask an adult to dictate the sentences clearly, in short phrases, and then check your answers together.

www

1 *Improve your spelling*

You will probably have had spellings to learn every week at school, so by Year 5 there will be many words that you can spell. No one is expecting you to be able to spell every word you write perfectly, but you do need to spell well enough to communicate in 11+ English.

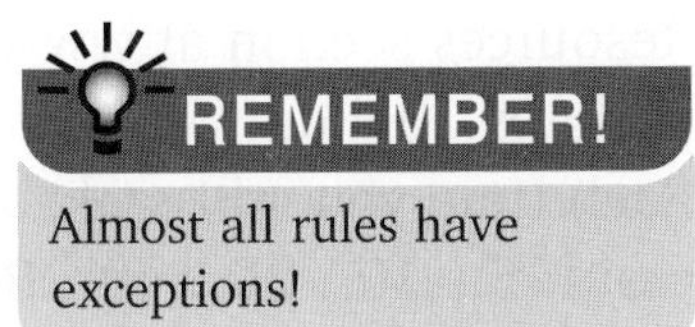
REMEMBER!
Almost all rules have exceptions!

Checklist

- ✓ Be aware of the most common spelling errors. (See page 77: Learn awkward spellings.)
- ✓ Learn the most important spelling rules, such as:
  - **'i' before 'e' except after 'c' if it sounds like 'eee'**;
  - **When two vowels go a-walking, the first vowel does the talking**.
- ✓ Practise spellings using **'look say cover write check'**.
- ✓ Set yourself challenges: choose ten new useful words a week to learn using a spelling list like *Schonell's Essential Spelling List*. (See inside cover for details.)
- ✓ Sound out words in syllables; make up rhymes; march to them or clap them. Spot syllables that are stressed and unstressed.
- ✓ When learning a new word, ask yourself:
  - Is it made up of familiar **smaller** words?
  - Does it have a common **letter string**?
  - Is it based on a common **root** word?
  - Does it have a **prefix** or **suffix** you recognise?
- ✓ Group words in your mind and on paper, according to their letter patterns, e.g. **–ight**, **–ur**, **–ous**, **–tion**.

continued overleaf

Checklist

- Spot and learn silent letters in words like 'i**s**land', 'crum**b**', '**k**nock' or 's**w**ord'.
- Try to make up **mnemonics** to help remember difficult words, for example '**b**irds **e**at **c**rumbs **a**s **u**ncle **s**its **e**ating' for 'because'.
- Get into the habit of using a dictionary, thesaurus or spellchecker to make sure that you have the right meaning and the right spelling.
- Practise spellings by enjoying wordsearches, crossword puzzles and word games.

REMEMBER!

Be interested in words and their spellings. Collect spellings of words you like and need to use.

"But there are thousands of words!"

Yes there are, so take it gradually.

To start with, make sure you can spell the top 100 basic words (see the Free Resources section at www.bond11plus.co.uk). Ask someone to test you on them, perhaps 20 a day. Write out five times any that you get wrong. Retest every day. Each time you still make an error, double the number of times you write out the word: 5…10…20…40…80… but you'll never need to write it out that many times!

PARENT TIP

Give your child regular spelling tests until he or she really knows these words. Help your child to compile lists of words that he or she finds especially difficult or wants to be able to use. These could be personal words, such as special names or places that are important to your family. Play word games like hangman using those words.

Work through the practice activities in the following sections to see what kinds of spellings you can do and which you need to look at more carefully and learn.

First, see how many of the 100 words you can remember.

Can you find and correct all the misspelt words in the passage that follows? Underline them and write the correct spellings in your exercise book. Check your answers against the list when you have finished. (There are 53 including repeat errors!)

Last year at crismas our familly had a speshul party with therty peepul. My arnt and unkel came with their two yung chilldren and our naybers from accross the road brort their sons aged therteen and forteen. My bruther's frend and his muther warked over from arownd the corner and meny uther frends and familly were there.

We had drinks bitwene harf past ten and noon folowed by delishus food. Dyouring lunch we sudenly herd a grate bang abuv the kitchen and sumthing crashed throo the window. We thort posibly the chimney had collapsed, but gradyerly realised the boys had tryed out a new football which had ferst bounced off the kitchen roof and then broken the window!

The boys imedyatly disapered before my farther toled them off and he yoused cardboard to mend the window. The hole party cood have been spoilt becos of this but one of our frends said at ferst he thort it was Farther crismas coming to join us which made everyone larf.

2 *Learn awkward spellings*

These are some of the most awkward sets of spellings you need to be aware of for 11+ English:

- homophones
- doubling letters
- one letter misplaced
- frequent culprits
- magic 'e'
- singulars and plurals
- common letter strings
- homonyms
- silent letters, unstressed vowels
- adding prefixes
- adding suffixes
- '-shun' suffixes

There is a section here on each of these with special hints and ideas for practice. Work through all the sections that you are unsure about or need to brush up on.

Homophones

Homophones are words that sound exactly the same but are spelt differently and have different meanings. There are hundreds of homophones. They come in pairs and sometimes in groups of three or even four.

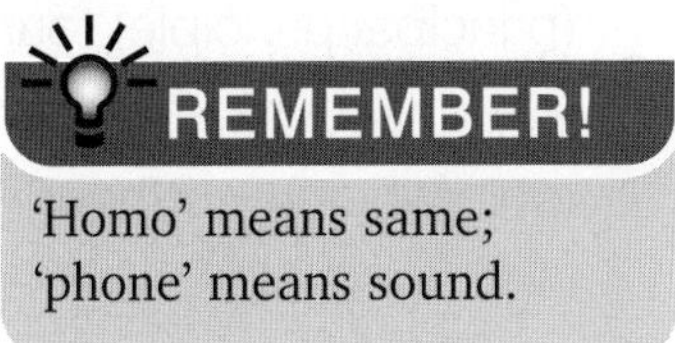
REMEMBER!
'Homo' means same;
'phone' means sound.

Here are some of the homophones that come up all the time and can cause confusion. People find them particularly tricky to spell because you have to be able to tell the difference between their meanings **and** spellings.

air/heir aloud/allowed are/our be/bee beech/beach board/bored by/buy/bye caught/court course/coarse current/currant for/four flower/flour great/grate hair/hare hole/whole its/it's key/quay led/lead main/mane new/knew not/knot no/know our/hour pale/pail past/passed practise/practice pray/prey principal/principle rain/reign/rein right/write/rite road/rode/rowed route/root saw/sore seen/scene serial/cereal so/sew/sow stationery/stationary sun/son their/there/they're through/threw thrown/throne tide/tied to/two/too waist/waste way/weigh week/weak where/wear which/witch whine/wine who's/whose would/wood you/ewe/yew you're/your

Pay special attention to learning homophones, both to their spellings and their meanings. It can help to:

Checklist

- ✓ draw pictures next to the ones you find especially confusing
- ✓ make up reminders like: stationery has the letter **'e'** for **e**nvelope in it.

Also look out for awkward homophones where one of the pair or group is spelt with an apostrophe. Be really careful about using these correctly.

Underline the correct homophones in this passage, thinking hard about the meaning each time.

Making (there/their/they're) (weigh/way) (through/threw) the (beach/beech) (would/wood) (which/witch) (lead/led) (to/too/two) the (main/mane)(beach/beech), Ahmed and Jack (new/knew) that they were only (aloud/allowed) (to/too/two) use the (root/route) that (past/passed) the golf (course/coarse) (where/wear) (there/their/they're) dads were having a (practise/practice) game before the (principal/principle) tournament of the season. The low (beach/beech) branches (caught/court) at (there/their/they're) (hair/hare) (so/sew/sow) it took them a (hole/whole) (our/hour) before they (saw/sore) the (course/coarse), (waist/waste)-high grass of the dunes.

Doubling letters

One of the most common spelling errors is forgetting to double a consonant when you need to keep the vowel sound short. Can you see which words have been spelt incorrectly in this sentence?

Jack was runing to put the rubish in the bin but at the begining of the drive he sudenly spoted a funy chuby rabit sliping out of its burow.

Here are some hints that can help to remind you when to double consonants:

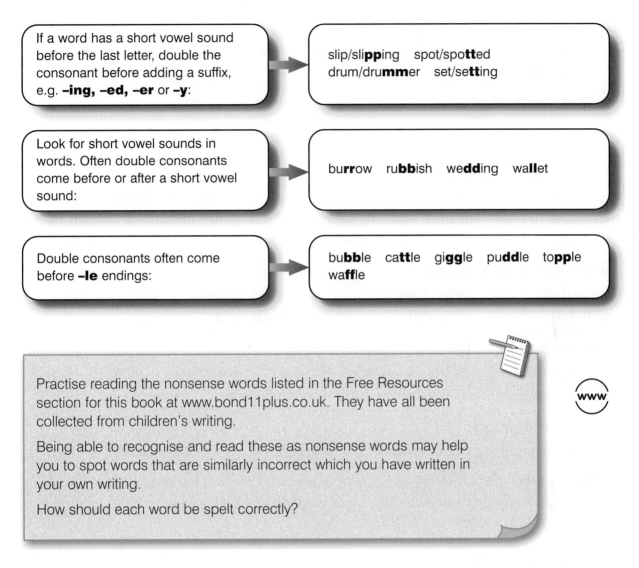

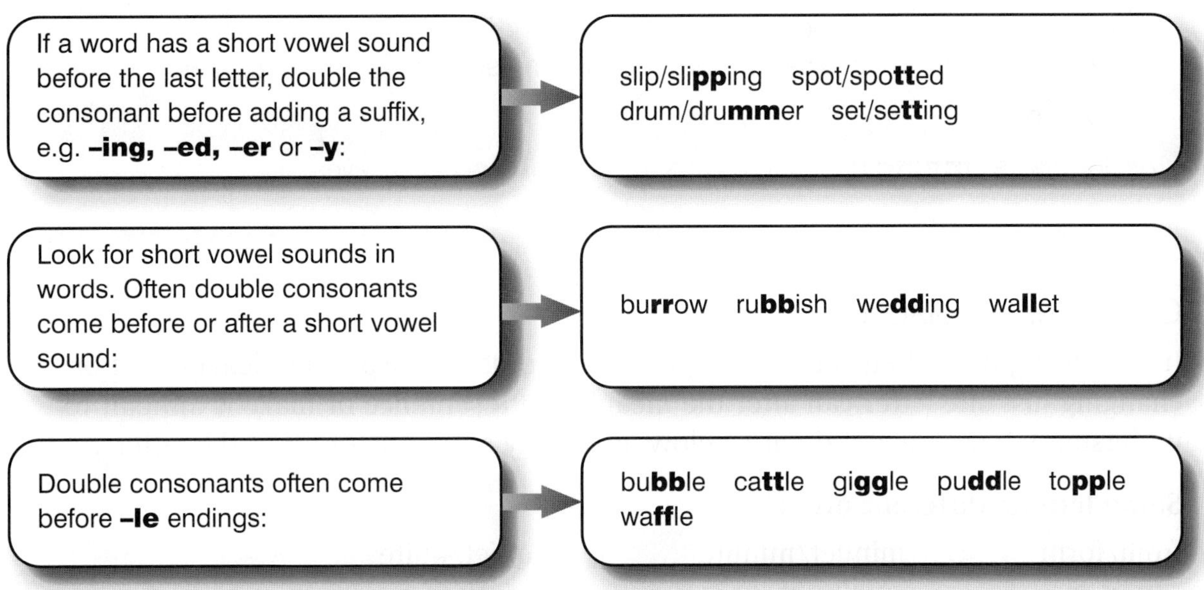

If a word has a short vowel sound before the last letter, double the consonant before adding a suffix, e.g. **-ing, -ed, -er** or **-y**:
slip/sli**pp**ing spot/spo**tt**ed drum/dru**mm**er set/se**tt**ing
Look for short vowel sounds in words. Often double consonants come before or after a short vowel sound:
bu**rr**ow ru**bb**ish we**dd**ing wa**ll**et
Double consonants often come before **-le** endings:
bu**bb**le ca**tt**le gi**gg**le pu**dd**le to**pp**le wa**ff**le

Practise reading the nonsense words listed in the Free Resources section for this book at www.bond11plus.co.uk. They have all been collected from children's writing.

Being able to recognise and read these as nonsense words may help you to spot words that are similarly incorrect which you have written in your own writing.

How should each word be spelt correctly?

Here are some examples of words where both versions with or without the doubled consonant make sense. Look out for pairs of words like these and add to the list if you can.

shinning/shining planned/planed sitting/siting hopping/hoping
pinning/pining holly/holy dinner/diner latter/later
comma/coma mopping/moping tapped/taped matting/mating
lopping/loping starring/staring ridding/riding barring/baring
slopped/sloped scarred/scared dessert/desert bidding/biding

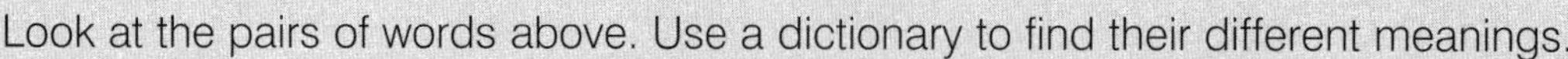

Look at the pairs of words above. Use a dictionary to find their different meanings.

Try to make up sentences that contain both words in the pairs below, so that you can clearly see what the words mean.

dessert/desert	dinner/diner	hopping/hoping	latter/later
planned/planed	scarred/scared	starring/staring	tapped/taped

For example:

As Joe was **shinning** up the tree the sun was **shining** in his eyes.

One letter misplaced

It is amazing how often some word pairs are confused. Misplacing, leaving out or changing just one letter can alter the meaning of a sentence or make it difficult to understand. Read the word pairs below and really study the order of the letters.

Same letters, different order:

from/form	minuet/minute	quiet/quite
split/spilt	trial/trail	untie/unite

One letter more or less:

country/county exciting/exiting first/fist learn/lean of/off
started/stared thorough/through through/though where/were

One letter different:

pointed/painted wander/wonder where/there effect/affect

Make sure that you check these kinds of words very thoroughly in your writing. Make up some funny sentences including these word pairs in your exercise book and add more pairs as you come across them.

Frequent culprits

There may be words that always seem to let you down. Here are some examples of words that can be frequent culprits:

answer	beautiful	busy	definitely	describe
design	excellent	favourite	February	friend
necessary	separate	special	tomorrow	usual

If these (or other words) constantly let you down, try to practise them every day until you know them. Make a poster of them for your room and get your family to test you regularly.

Magic 'e'

Be aware of how the letter 'e' can completely change one word to make another by changing a short vowel sound into a long vowel sound. Look at the examples below, which show how magic 'e' works. Say each pair aloud and listen to the difference the magic 'e' makes to the way you pronounce the words.

bar/bare   cloth/clothe   grim/grime   kit/kite
pin/pine   quit/quite   rod/rode   scar/scare
scrap/scrape   slid/slide   spit/spite   star/stare   strip/stripe

When the letter 'e' is at the end of a word, it doesn't always change the sound of the vowel. With many ancient words, such as: '**come**', '**some**', '**gone**' and all the words ending in a '**v**' sound, such as: '**have**', '**give**', '**love**', '**above**', '**twelve**', the final 'e' doesn't make a long vowel sound.

Notice the effect magic 'e' can also have on the letter '**g**' in these word pairs:

hug/ huge   rag/rage   stag/stage   wag/wage

It makes a long vowel sound but also makes the letter 'g' soft so that it sounds like '**j**'. Here are some other words where magic 'e' affects the vowel and the letter 'g':

age   agent   courage   danger   digest   strange   stranger

Magic 'e' can have a similar effect on the letter '**c**', too. When a 'c' is followed by an 'e' it changes to a soft, hissing '**ss**' sound. Here are some words where magic 'e' affects the vowel and the letter 'c':

ace   brace   disgrace   face   grace
lace   pace   place   race   replace
space   trace   dice   ice   lice
mice   nice   price   rice   slice
spice   twice   vice   puce   truce

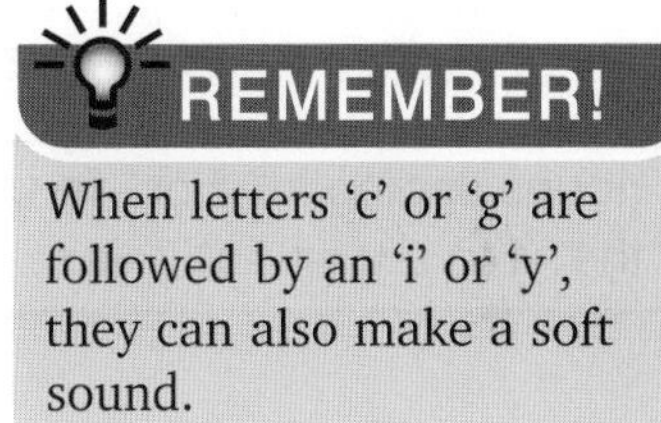

REMEMBER!
When letters 'c' or 'g' are followed by an 'i' or 'y', they can also make a soft sound.

Some words have both a hard and soft 'c' sound:

accident   access   concert   success

Practise reading and learn to spell words which contain a soft 'g' or a soft 'c' followed by 'e', 'i' or 'y'. Here are some to get you started.

acid   bicycle   cinema   circle   circumstance   civil
icicle   pencil   recipe   apology   gorgeous   apologise
energy   engine   fringe   fragile   gentle   gesture
gigantic   ginger   gym   magic   orange   origin
pigeon   region   religion   surgeon   suggest

Always be careful when adding 'e' to words and remember all the ways it can change letter sounds.

Singulars and plurals

You need to know how to make nouns plural. Many spelling errors at 11+ English are made by forming incorrect plurals. There are some simple rules you can learn.

Singular means **one**; plural means **more than one**.

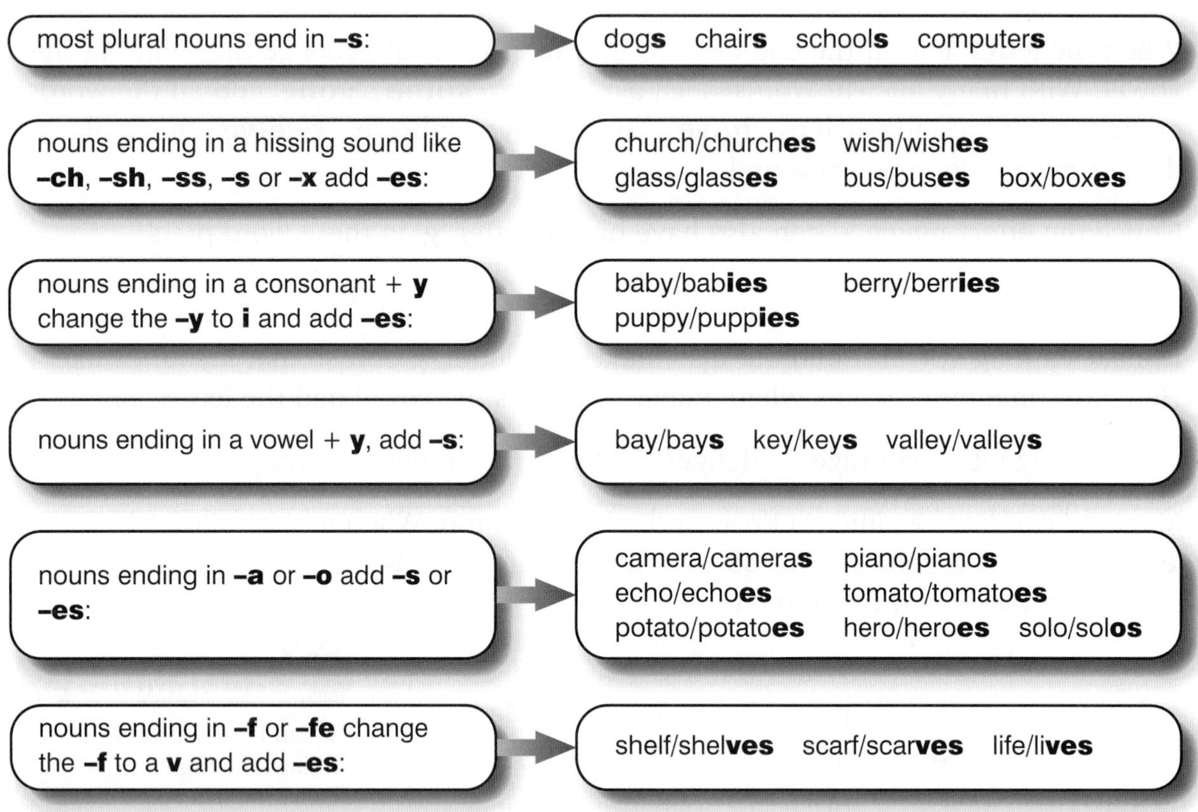

most plural nouns end in **–s**:
dog**s** chair**s** school**s** computer**s**
nouns ending in a hissing sound like **–ch**, **–sh**, **–ss**, **–s** or **–x** add **–es**:
church/church**es** wish/wish**es** glass/glass**es** bus/bus**es** box/box**es**
nouns ending in a consonant + **y** change the **–y** to **i** and add **–es**:
baby/bab**ies** berry/berr**ies** puppy/pupp**ies**
nouns ending in a vowel + **y**, add **–s**:
bay/bay**s** key/key**s** valley/valley**s**
nouns ending in **–a** or **–o** add **–s** or **–es**:
camera/camera**s** piano/piano**s** echo/echo**es** tomato/tomato**es** potato/potato**es** hero/hero**es** solo/solo**s**
nouns ending in **–f** or **–fe** change the **–f** to a **v** and add **–es**:
shelf/shel**ves** scarf/scar**ves** life/li**ves**

REMEMBER!

There are some exceptions to this last rule which just add **-s**. These also need to be learnt:

chef/chefs
belief/beliefs
chief/chiefs
handkerchief/handkerchiefs

Look out for words that have **irregular** plurals, e.g.:

sheep/sheep	ox/oxen
salmon/salmon	child/children
woman/women	man/men
tooth/teeth	foot/feet
mouse/mice	trousers/trousers

Make collections of words that obey all of these different plurals' rules.

Common letter strings

Many words share the same common letter strings but some spelling patterns can be a little harder to learn. Learning and recognising these patterns can help you to say and spell unfamiliar words.

Some of the more challenging spelling patterns are shown in the tables that follow. Collect words that contain these common letter strings, looking out for homophones, and make collections in your exercise book for each group. Remember to look out for exceptions!

Sounds like 'er'		
er	ir	ur
her	bird	purse
certain	first	curl
term		

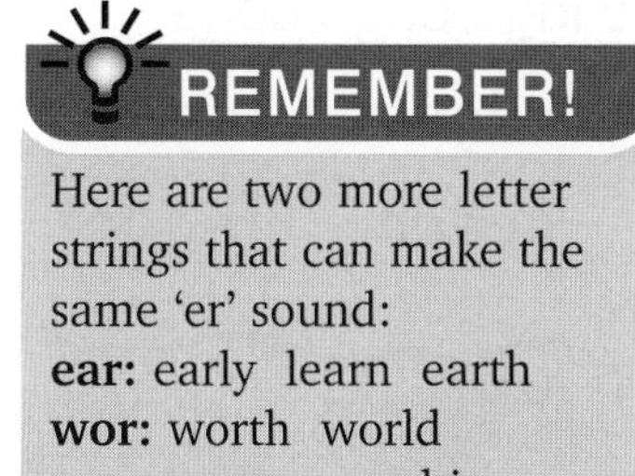

REMEMBER!

Here are two more letter strings that can make the same 'er' sound:
ear: early learn earth
wor: worth world worm worship

Sounds like 'or'						
au	augh	aw	oar	oor	or	our
author	daughter	awful	soar	door	for	four
haul	taught	crawl	board	floor	story	court

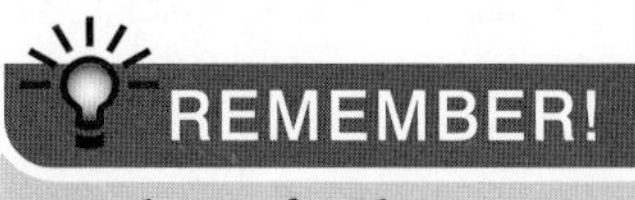

REMEMBER!

Watch out for these exceptions: laugh, draught

REMEMBER!

Here are some more letter strings that can make the same 'or' sound:
ar: quarter
war: warm ('**w**' often changes the vowel sound in words)
See also the table for letter string '**ough**'.

atch/etch/itch/otch/utch				
atch	etch	itch	otch	utch
batch	fetch	ditch	blotch	hutch
		kitchen		

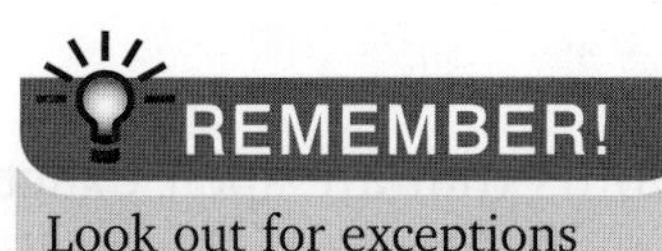

REMEMBER!

Look out for exceptions such as:
att**ach** r**ich** sandw**ich** wh**ich** m**uch** s**uch** t**ouch**

ack/eck/ick/ock/uck				
ack	eck	ick	ock	uck
lack	peck	pick	sock	luck
		sticker		

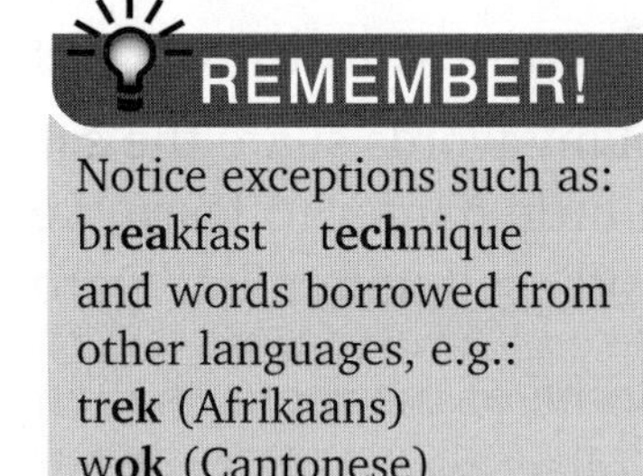

REMEMBER!

Notice exceptions such as:
br**ea**kfast te**ch**nique
and words borrowed from other languages, e.g.:
trek (Afrikaans)
wok (Cantonese)

adge/edge/idge/odge/udge				
adge	edge	idge	odge	udge
badge	hedge	fridge	dodge	fudge

This next letter string can be especially tricky, as it is pronounced very differently in different words.

ough							
Sounds like:	off	oh	oo	or	ow	uff	uh
	cough	dough	through	thought	bough	tough	borough

cious/tious/xious		
cious	tious	xious
suspicious	cautious	anxious
vicious		

Homonyms

These are words that are spelt exactly the same but have different meanings. Some are pronounced differently depending on their meanings.

Homonyms can cause confusion for readers. Sometimes you have to stress different syllables or change the vowel sounds to make the meanings clear. Look at the examples of homonyms given below.

Same pronunciation

bark/bark	block/block	club/club	fly/fly	form/form
jam/jam	leaves/leaves	train/train	watch/watch	waves/waves

Can you work out a different meaning for each word in these pairs? Here are some sentences that show the different meanings of three of these homonym pairs:

Sam watched the **fly fly** past the window.

He was making a **bark** rubbing when his dog began to **bark**.

I ate a **jam** sandwich while sitting in the traffic **jam**.

REMEMBER!

These same pronunciation homonyms are often different parts of speech. (See page 58.)

Different pronunciation

bow/bow	conduct/conduct	desert/desert	lead/lead
live/live	minute/minute	perfect/perfect	present/present
read/read	row/row	sow/sow	tear/tear
wind/wind	wound/wound		

Do you know how each of these homonyms is pronounced? Here are some sentences that show the different meanings of three of these homonym pairs:

The guide will **lead** you to the **lead** mine.

In a **minute** you will hear a **minute** splash as the stone hits the bottom of the well.

The nurse **wound** a bandage around the boy's **wound**.

Make up sentences that clearly show the different meanings of homonyms, like the example sentences above.

Look out for homonyms in your reading and build up a collection of homonyms in your exercise book. Write sentences to show the different meanings.

Silent letters and unstressed vowels

There are many words in English which have silent letters or unstressed vowels in them and you will need to pay particular attention to these, because simply sounding them out will not help you to spell them correctly.

Here are some of the most common **silent letters**, with some handy hints that can help you think about where these letters can appear. Some useful silent letter words are given for each letter, but there are many more, so look out for them in your reading and writing.

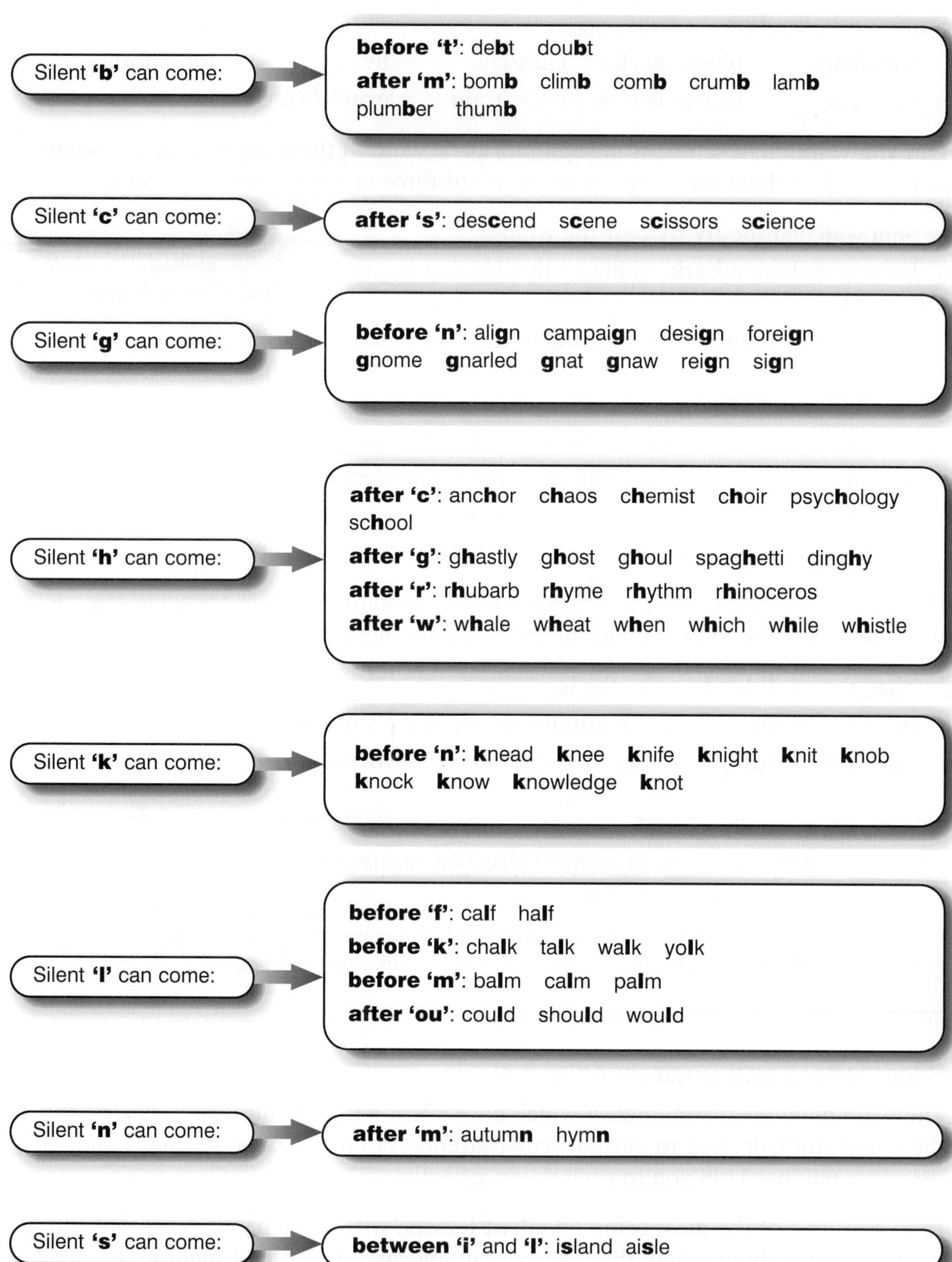
Silent **'b'** can come:
before 't': de**b**t dou**b**t
after 'm': bom**b** clim**b** com**b** crum**b** lam**b** plum**b**er thum**b**
Silent **'c'** can come:
after 's': des**c**end s**c**ene s**c**issors s**c**ience
Silent **'g'** can come:
before 'n': ali**g**n campai**g**n desi**g**n forei**g**n **g**nome **g**narled **g**nat **g**naw rei**g**n si**g**n
Silent **'h'** can come:
after 'c': anc**h**or c**h**aos c**h**emist c**h**oir psyc**h**ology sc**h**ool
after 'g': g**h**astly g**h**ost g**h**oul spag**h**etti ding**h**y
after 'r': r**h**ubarb r**h**yme r**h**ythm r**h**inoceros
after 'w': w**h**ale w**h**eat w**h**en w**h**ich w**h**ile w**h**istle
Silent **'k'** can come:
before 'n': **k**nead **k**nee **k**nife **k**night **k**nit **k**nob **k**nock **k**now **k**nowledge **k**not
Silent **'l'** can come:
before 'f': ca**l**f ha**l**f
before 'k': cha**l**k ta**l**k wa**l**k yo**l**k
before 'm': ba**l**m ca**l**m pa**l**m
after 'ou': cou**l**d shou**l**d wou**l**d
Silent **'n'** can come:
after 'm': autum**n** hym**n**
Silent **'s'** can come:
between 'i' and 'l': i**s**land ai**s**le

Silent **'t'** can come:

before –le ending: cas**t**le rus**t**le this**t**le wres**t**le

before –en ending: chris**t**en fas**t**en glis**t**en lis**t**en mois**t**en sof**t**en

at the end of foreign words: balle**t** chale**t**

Silent **'w'** can come:

before 'r': **w**rap **w**reath **w**reck **w**ren **w**riggle **w**rinkle **w**rist **w**rite **w**rong **w**rote

after 's': answer sword

REMEMBER!

Making up **mnemonics** (short sentences, rhymes or silly stories) can help you remember the silent and unstressed letters in words. For instance:

Lucy is at the back of the castle. Noel stood at the back to sing the hymn.
or
The **w**rinkled **w**ren **w**riggled on the **w**recked **w**reath.

Trace over the silent letters with a silver pen!

Unstressed vowels are not sounded clearly:

benefit (the second 'e' sounds like **'uh'**)

Often they are not pronounced at all:

medicine (the first **'i'** is often **'swallowed'**)

Read these examples of the two types aloud. Listen to what happens to the unstressed vowels. (They are highlighted in bold.)

'uh' vowels:

astron**o**my dand**e**lion gramm**a**r sim**i**lar tel**e**phone

'swallowed' vowels:

jewell**e**ry fact**o**ry short**e**ning int**e**rest mini**a**ture fam**i**ly

REMEMBER!

Unstressed vowels often come in words that contain the letter patterns **'en'** or **'er'**.

Find the unstressed vowels in each of these words and highlight them.

boundary	business	conference	dangerous	definitely
dictionary	different	easily	extraordinary	eventually
favourite	generous	glamorous	heaven	history
humorous	interesting	jewellery	naturally	occasionally

Look out for unstressed vowels as you read.

Adding prefixes

You need to know the meanings of some of the most common prefixes as they may help you to understand the meanings of some unfamiliar words. Not all prefixes have particular meanings but you should know the most common ones:

A prefix is a group of letters added to the beginning of a word to change its meaning.

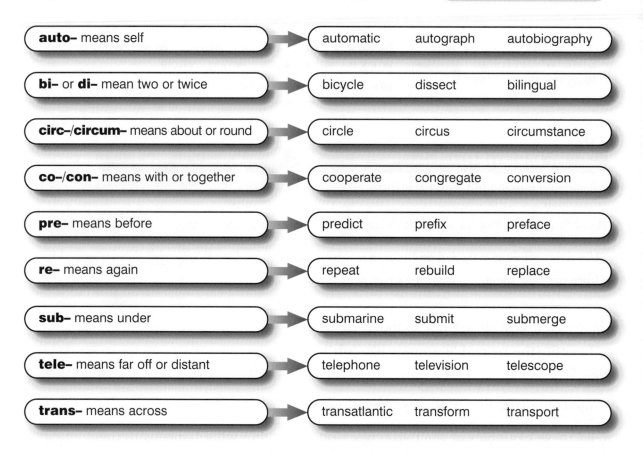

auto– means self	automatic	autograph	autobiography
bi– or **di–** mean two or twice	bicycle	dissect	bilingual
circ–/circum– means about or round	circle	circus	circumstance
co–/con– means with or together	cooperate	congregate	conversion
pre– means before	predict	prefix	preface
re– means again	repeat	rebuild	replace
sub– means under	submarine	submit	submerge
tele– means far off or distant	telephone	television	telescope
trans– means across	transatlantic	transform	transport

These prefixes are all used to make **antonyms** (opposites). (See page 65.)

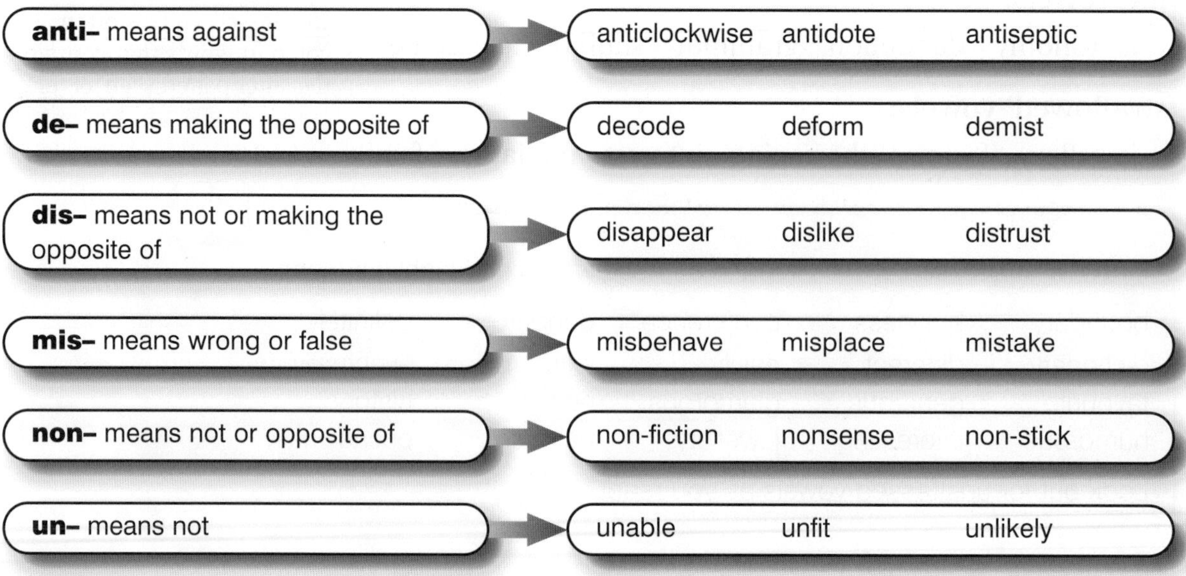

anti– means against	anticlockwise	antidote	antiseptic
de– means making the opposite of	decode	deform	demist
dis– means not or making the opposite of	disappear	dislike	distrust
mis– means wrong or false	misbehave	misplace	mistake
non– means not or opposite of	non-fiction	nonsense	non-stick
un– means not	unable	unfit	unlikely

In your exercise book, collect as many words with these and other prefixes as you can and make sure you know what they all mean.

Notice that the same root words can have different prefixes and then mean quite different things.

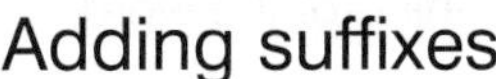

Adding suffixes

You need to know the most common suffixes:

–able **–ed** **–er** **–est** **–ful** **–ing**
–less **–ly** **–ment** **–tion**

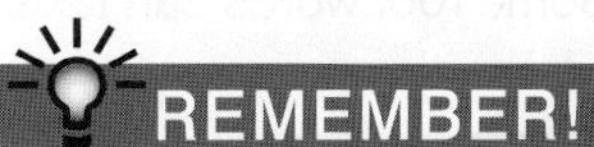

A suffix is a group of letters added to the end of a word to change its meaning.

Some of these can be added without changing the spelling of the root word (e.g. **–ful**, **–less**, **–ment**) but sometimes changes to the root word are needed. Here are some general rules which can help you to work out what these changes are and when they are needed. Remember: most rules have exceptions!

Remember the rule for adding suffixes to words that end in 'e':
Ends in 'e', delete the 'e'!

For suffixes beginning with an **'a'**, **'e'** or **'i'**:
If the root ends with an 'e', drop the 'e' then add the suffix.

If the root ends with a short vowel sound followed by a single consonant, double the consonant then add the suffix: (See Doubling letters, page 78.)

shop → shop**ped** shop**per** shop**ping**

For suffixes **–er**, **–est**, **–ly** or **–ness**:
If the root ends with a **'y'**, change the **'y'** to **'i'** then add the suffix.

For the suffix **–tion**:
If the root ends with an **'e'**, drop the **'e'** then add the suffix:

If the root ends with **'t'** or **'te'**, drop these letters then add the suffix:

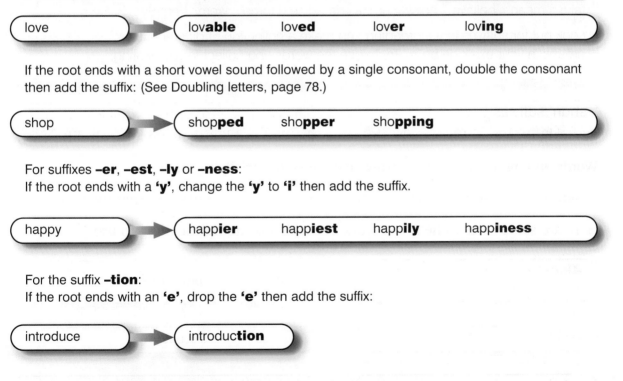

Some root endings will need to be changed further:

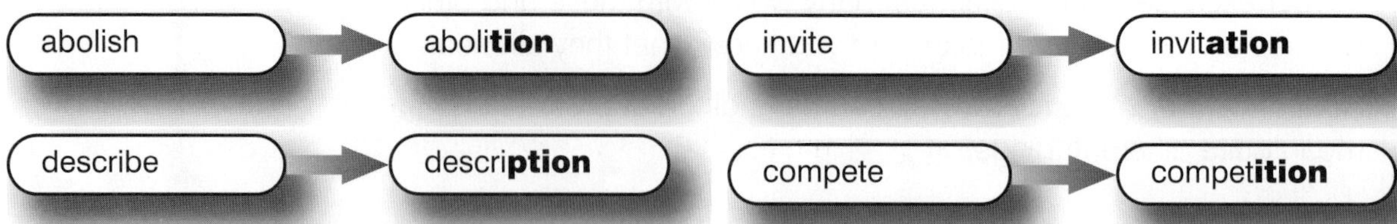

Some root words can take several different suffixes. Each suffix changes the meaning of the word.

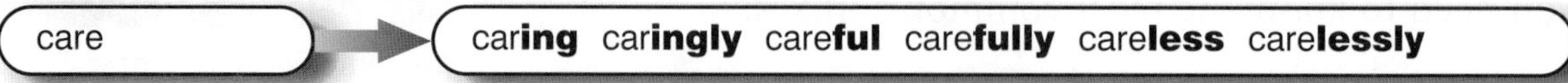

Sometimes the **'e'** at the end of a root word needs to be kept before adding a suffix or else the meaning is changed. Notice what happens to these words if you drop the **'e'**:

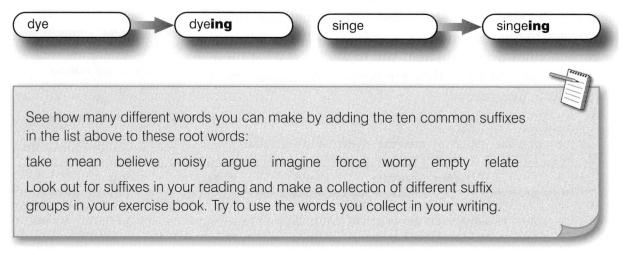

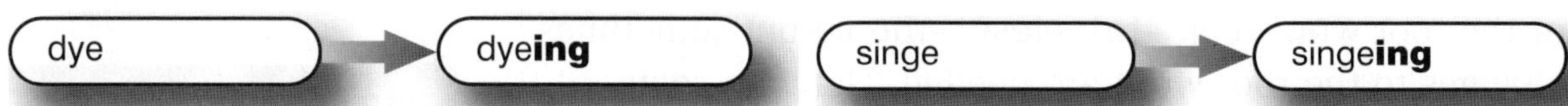

See how many different words you can make by adding the ten common suffixes in the list above to these root words:

take mean believe noisy argue imagine force worry empty relate

Look out for suffixes in your reading and make a collection of different suffix groups in your exercise book. Try to use the words you collect in your writing.

'–shun' suffixes

Several different suffixes make the same 'shun' sound but they are all spelt differently.

Words ending in these letter strings can be rather tricky to spell:

–tion –ssion –cian –sion (this one often sounds a bit different from the others!)

Here are some rules to help you work out which is the right ending to use:

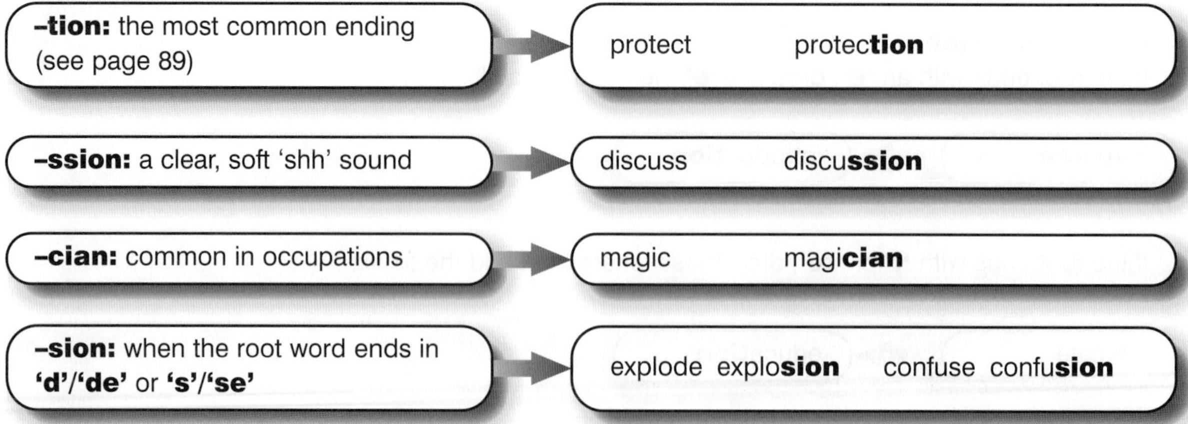

–tion: the most common ending (see page 89)
protect protec**tion**
–ssion: a clear, soft 'shh' sound
discuss discu**ssion**
–cian: common in occupations
magic magi**cian**
–sion: when the root word ends in **'d'**/**'de'** or **'s'**/**'se'**
explode explo**sion** confuse confu**sion**

Sort these words into their suffix groups:

competition	devotion	translation	extension	possession
explanation	direction	profession	fiction	collision
optician	demonstration	musician	electrician	television
politician				

Make a collection of **'shun'** words. Add more words to the groups as you come across them in your reading. Split them into syllables to make learning their spellings easier.

3 *Practise the skills!*

Now have a go at putting the spelling rules you have learnt into practice by doing a dictation test. You will need to ask an adult to read out the sentences from the dictation test located in the Free Resources section for this book at www.bond11plus.co.uk. See how many words you are able to spell! If you tried this dictation test before working through Section E, compare your scores to check what you have learnt.

F How do you prepare for the exam?

1 What next?

You've worked through this book. Now test yourself!

If you used the central pull-out test before reading this book, have another go at it now and see how you have improved. For more practice, and to put your skills to the test, work through the range of books and test papers in the *Bond 11+ English* range.

Mark your answers with an adult. Talk about the questions you got wrong or found hard to understand. Read the sections in this book again to help brush up on things you are still not sure about.

Ask a parent or teacher to comment on your story-writing, presentation and comprehension answers.

2 Build confidence with practice

It is a good idea to go over examples of things that might come up in an 11+ English exam well before the date. A useful way to do this is to try some English tests that are similar to the exam you will be doing. The *Bond* papers used regularly, perhaps once a fortnight during Year 5 and Year 6 term-time weeks and once a week during the holidays, will provide useful, graded practice that will build your confidence and show you how well you cope with doing tests of this kind.

PARENT TIP

For more advice on practice routines and useful techniques, read The Parents' Guide to the 11+. *See inside cover for more details.*

3 Time yourself

If you are just starting to prepare yourself, you may find it helpful to whizz through your first few *Bond Assessment Papers in English* untimed. This will help you to familiarise yourself with the types of questions and tasks you will face in the exam. Note down your scores (you could use the progress grids at the back of the *Bond Assessment Papers*) and be sure to go over all the questions you found difficult until you understand them. After that, though, it is very important to give yourself a set time, just as you will have in the exam, so that you can practise pacing yourself and aiming to complete everything in the given time.

PARENT TIP

Remember to be encouraging and positive about what your child produces! If there are mistakes or some parts still cause difficulty, that's quite natural; no one's perfect!

4 Revise strategies and techniques

It is also worth thinking about exam strategies and techniques. For many children, 11+ exams are the first exams they do in their lives, and they get very nervous at the thought of them. So do their parents! There are lots of hints on strategies and techniques in this book. Flick through them and talk about them to remind yourself. It may be a good idea to make a reminder list of things to particularly look out for in the exam.

It is very important to remember that everyone is different. You will have your own way of coping and of doing things which may be quite different from the way other people work. If you have worked through this book, you will have a good idea of your own strengths and weaknesses, the things you find easy or difficult. You will have developed your own strategies and techniques in tests and in your learning.

5 The exam day itself

"I'm so nervous..."

Of course you may be nervous, but actually, when it comes to the day, many people find they can enjoy their exams, as long as they feel confident and well prepared. After all, you will have done all the practice; now it's your chance to show what you can do!

Just before the exam

Here are some useful things to remember before the exam day arrives:

Checklist

- ✓ Don't worry about feeling a bit nervous; that's natural. Most children will feel anxious. Talk about your feelings and try to relax.
- ✓ Plan something fun to do after the exam is over.
- ✓ Try to have a good night's sleep.

On the day

Checklist

- ✓ Eat a healthy breakfast and have something to drink.
- ✓ Get to the place where the exam is happening in plenty of time.
- ✓ Find out where the toilets are and go if you can before the exam starts.

In the exam room

There should be no distractions during the exam because everyone is in the same boat as you and there will be at least one adult making sure that everything runs smoothly. The adult will also tell you when to start, when to stop and will keep an eye on you all so that, for instance, there is no cheating.

Here are some useful strategies and techniques to remember once you are in the exam room:

Checklist

- ✓ **Keep calm.** If you get butterflies or feel anxious, sit up straight, make sure your shoulders are not hunched and take some deep breaths. This allows plenty of oxygen to get to your brain, which needs it!
- ✓ **Think positive.** You've done all the hard work preparing. Now enjoy yourself!
- ✓ **Find the clock.** Make sure you know where it is before you start, so you can do a time-check during the exam.
- ✓ **Read the question.** Not doing so is the most common mistake and easy to do something about.
- ✓ **Write careful answers.** Again, most mistakes are careless ones or 'kick yourself' mistakes.
- ✓ **Show what you know.** This is your big moment and what you've practised for. Try to enjoy showing what you have learnt.
- ✓ **If you can't do a question, don't panic:** have a go. Write something, and then put a mark in the margin, showing that you need to have another look if you have time at the end. Remember: a blank scores zero; a good guess may well be right.
- ✓ **Leave time to check.** Remember to leave a few minutes to check through your answers and make sure they make sense.
- ✓ **Do your best:** you can't do better than that!

GOOD LUCK!

Glossary

abbreviation – a shortened version of a word or phrase.

abstract noun – a concept or idea; something that cannot be seen, heard or touched.

acronym – the first letters of words put together as a short version and said as a single word.

active – where someone or something is actually doing something.

adjective – a word used to describe a noun.

adverb – a word used to describe a verb.

alphabetical order – words or letters put in the order in which they would come in the alphabet.

antonym – a word with an opposite meaning to another word.

auxiliary verbs – parts of the verbs ' to be' or 'to have' which go with other verbs to help make a tense.

character – a person in a story, play script or other kind of narrative text.

cliffhanger – an ending to a story or piece of writing which leaves the reader guessing about what may happen next.

collective noun – a word that stands for a group or collection of things.

comparative adjective – a word that is used to compare two things.

complex – a more complicated version of something.

compound word – two or more words put together to make a new idea.

conditional – perhaps or maybe, where one thing depends upon another.

conjunction – a word used to join together two or more sentences.

connective – a word or phrase used to join together two or more sentences.

contraction – when two or more words are joined together to make just one word, using apostrophes to show any missing letters, e.g. do not = don't.

dialogue – a conversation between two or more characters in a story.

dictate – read words aloud so that someone else can write them down.

dilemma – a problem which needs to be solved.

diminutive – a small or young version of something or somebody.

direct speech – the actual words people say to each other.

double negative – saying no twice, so that it means yes.

exception – a word which does not follow common rules and needs to be learnt separately.

feedback – advice and comments given by someone else in response to a piece of writing.

feminine – female, like a girl or a woman.

first person – using 'I' or 'we'.

formal – following rules; polite.

gender – tells whether something is male or female.

homonym – a word that sounds the same as another and is spelt the same but has a different meaning.

homophone – a word that sounds the same as another but has a different meaning and is spelt differently.

imagery – words used to bring pictures into the reader's mind.

indefinite pronoun – a word that stands for a noun but not a particular one, e.g. everything/something/anything, etc.

indent – a way to show the beginning of a paragraph where the first line of writing begins a little further to the right of the margin than the other lines.

infer – work out meaning from the clues in a text, even though the exact meaning is not given.

infinitive – the name of a verb.

informal – being relaxed and chatty.

introduction – the beginning of a piece of writing, setting the scene or introducing characters or ideas.

irregular – does not follow the usual rules.

Latin – an old language spoken by the Romans over two thousand years ago which forms the root of many of our English words.

legibly – writing in a way which can be read easily.

letter string – letters that commonly go together to make certain sounds.

main clause – part of a sentence which contains a verb.

margin – a blank border at the left-hand side of a page.

masculine – male, like a boy or a man.

metaphor – a phrase used to describe something as if it was something else.

mnemonic – a way of remembering things which are difficult to remember.

moral – a lesson that stories like fables teach a reader.

narrator – the person telling the story.

negative – saying no or not.

noun – a naming word.

object – who or what is being affected by the subject and the verb in a sentence.

onomatopoeia – words that sound the same as their meanings.

paragraph – a sentence or set of sentences describing one stage of a piece of writing, separated from the next paragraph either by a line space or an indent.

passive – where someone or something is having something done to them.

personal pronoun – a word that stands for a noun and shows who, e.g. I/me, we/us, they/them, etc.

persuasive writing – a piece of writing which tries to make the reader share a point of view.

phrase – a group of words which has a meaning but is not a complete sentence.

plot – the problem or dilemma developed in a story.

plural – more than one.

positive – saying yes or definitely.

possessive pronoun – a word that stands for a noun and shows to whom it belongs, e.g. mine, yours, his, hers, etc.

predict – decide what may happen next, using clues in the text to support what you say.

prefix – a group of letters added in front of a root word to change its meaning.

preposition – a word that shows the position, direction or timing of a noun.

presentation – the way a piece of writing looks.

pronoun – a word used instead of a noun: he, it, they, we, you, she, I, etc.

pronunciation – how you say a word.

proper noun – a special name (or title) of a person, place or thing.

prose – a piece of continuous writing.

proverb – a wise saying, often very old.

recount – a retelling of a series of events.

relative pronoun – a word that stands for a noun and tells more about it.

reported (indirect) speech – what people say to each other, but not in the actual words they use.

rhyming words – words which end with the same sound.

root word – the main part of a word to which prefixes and/or suffixes can be added.

sentence – a group of words that go together to make sense, usually starting with a capital letter and ending with a full stop.

silent letter – a letter that cannot be heard in a spoken word.

simile – a phrase used to compare one thing with another using 'like' or 'as … as'.

singular – only one.

Standard English – a form of English which is used as a guide for good English.

strategy – a way of working out a problem.

structure – the shape of a piece of writing and how it is organised.

subject – who or what is doing the action of the verb in a sentence.

subordinate clause – part of a sentence but does not contain a verb.

suffix – a group of letters added after a root word to change its meaning.

superlative adjective – a word that is used to describe the most, the biggest, the best, the worst, etc.

syllable – part of a word that contains at least one vowel and makes one sound.

synonym – a word with a similar meaning to another word.

technique – a way of doing things.

tense – used to show if a verb is in the past, present or future.

third person – using 'he', 'she' or 'they'.

topic – something to write, learn or talk about.

unstressed vowel – a vowel that is not clear when a word is spoken.

verb – an action word that shows doing, having or being.

vocabulary – the range of words that a person knows and can use.

Answers

B: Comprehension

(The answers to the standard questions are only possible answers. The adult working with the child will have to decide whether the child's answers show understanding of the text and the questions.)

3 Be aware of different text types

(practice box, page 9)

a) informative/explanatory
b) narrative
c) description
d) poem
e) instructions

5 Practise the skills!

(page 11)

A Tom Sawyer

Standard

1 Tom was in despair because time was moving so slowly. He thought it must be nearly daylight when it was only 10 p.m.
2 Ticking of a clock; cracking of old beams; creaking of stairs; Aunt Polly's snores; a cricket chirping; the ticking of a death-watch beetle; the howling of dogs.
3 The death-watch beetle's ticking meant that someone was going to die soon.
4 A cat was 'singing' or caterwauling and someone in a neighbouring house shouted and threw a bottle at the cat to make it stop.
5 a) find b) forever/endless time c) mixing

Multiple-choice

1 he was afraid of waking Sid
2 recognisable
3 small sounds made him think of ghosts
4 Tom was sleeping lightly
5 mixing
6 a neighbour
7 another dog's distant response
8 it was impossible for anyone to find the cricket by using its sound

B The Fawn

1 Any three of: polished cleft small ebony hooves; spotty and plain to see; jointy knees; new legs
2 The fawn was lying 'plain to see on the green moss' so that anyone could find him; he wasn't hidden or camouflaged.
3 The poet would have liked to be friends for one moment only, at least.
4 'seen without surprise'
5 crashing, leaping, stumbling
6 a) retrieve b) knees c) above
7 cleft = split dappled = spotted

C Hammerhead Sharks

1 bonnethead, winged hammerhead, scalloped hammerhead
2 nine
3 warm temperate and tropical coastal waters
4 undersea peaks, sea mounts
5 The hammerhead's head can be half as long as its body
6 all together
7 scalloped hammerhead
8 when the light fades
9 a) school b) projections c) dawn d) congregate

D Painted Pots

1 an art supplier's
2 soak up water easily
3 mixing paint with water
4 the pattern is transferred onto the pot
5 make a double pattern
6 the colour of the paint is pale
7 completely; discarded; lined-up; copy

E Ant's Pants

1 The two boys are in town to go shopping for a shirt for Ant.
2 Marlon thinks that school discos are rubbish/pathetic.
3 Marlon's mum turned up at 9 p.m. to collect him from the last school disco and it was announced over the microphone by Fungus, which really embarrassed Marlon.
4 Marlon is imitating the sound of Fungus's ancient, old-fashioned records.
5 Ant is looking forward to the disco as he has been practising an impressive dance routine.
6 **A** ancient: old/out-of-date
B pathetic: sad/weak **C** mega: amazing
D gear: outfit/clothes
7 The words in italics are stage directions.
8 **A** because **B** microphone **C** yes
9 They have been used to show the way that the boys talk in informal slang.
10 Ant has been showing off with his dance. A bighead means a 'show-off'.

C: Writing

4 *Improve your writing*

(practice box, page 31)

a) In the second version of the story you are told: the bird is a sparrow; he hopped confidently; his head bobbed as he pecked for crumbs; his eyes were alert and attentive; the bird screeched as it flew away.
b) The first version doesn't say Billy: was sitting under a holly bush; was a marmalade tomcat; was sitting in a hunched position; was almost coiled like a spring; had a stiff tail; had yellow eyes; sat down after he missed the bird; was disappointed that the bird got away; had a feather trapped under his left paw.

Add imagery *(Dylan Thomas extract, page 40)*

Similes: fill every inch of the hot little house like an old buffalo squeezed into an airing cupboard; his braces straining like hawsers; breathing like a brass band.

Metaphors: he was so big and trumpeting; she whisked about on padded claws; feeding the buffalo; to squeak in a nook or nibble in the hayloft; a steaming hulk; the great black boats of his boots; the loud checked meadow of his waistcoat; the forest fire of his hair

Think about the senses *(Laurie Lee extract, page 41)*

Sense words or phrases: scooped the dust; we slid through the grass; stared at the empty sky; Small heated winds blew; dandelion seeds floated by; burnt sap and roast nettles tingled our nostrils; the dull rust smell of dry ground; humming with blundering bees; flickering with scarlet butterflies.

D: Grammar and punctuation

1 Sentences

(practice box, page 50)

But they were not listening, none of them were. **T**hey were staring out over the sea, a look of utter astonishment on every face. **T**here was nothing there but the sound at first, a curious roaring and crying from the open sea beyond Popplestones that became a crescendo of thunderous snorting and whistling. **W**ithin minutes Popplestones was alive with whales. **G**reat spouts of water shot into the air. **E**verywhere you looked in the bay shining black backs broke the surface, rocked a little and then rolled forward and vanished again under the water. **A**ll of Big Tim's friends had already fled up the beach, but he stayed with us, mesmerised as we were. **B**eside us, the stranded whale writhed and rolled in its grave of sand, its tail thrashing in fury and frustration, its own whistling cry joining the chorus of the others out in Popplestones.

2 Phrases and clauses

(practice box, page 52)

a) sc b) p c) sc d) mc e) p f) sc g) mc h) mc i) p

(practice box, page 53)

connectives in A: and; so; until

phrases in B: dressed in shorts; in the crystal blue pool; taking a deep breath; dragging himself to even colder water; All of a sudden

main clauses in C: Jim was swimming; the water was freezing; He ... dived; his head grazed the bottom

subordinate clauses in C: while his dad was fishing; Although the sun was shining; Even though the pool was deep

connectives in C: while; Although; Even though

4 Commas

(practice box, page 55)

The children rehearsed their play several times, finding that it was becoming a smoother, more successful performance. Jim, pleased with the progress they were making, decided to call for a break. "Let's grab a bite from the kitchen," he suggested, "and then, if you like, we can go out for some fresh air, exercise and a change of scene."

The others agreed and Alan, suddenly remembering he had promised to phone his mother, made a quick phone call. "It's going really well, Mum," he said. "Tell Dad, Giles, Uncle Bob and Ellie to be ready for six o'clock."

6 Parts of speech

(practice box, page 62)

red pen:

1 James; Aunt Fanny; Arnold; Rector; Thomas Kempe

2 normal; ordinary; football; proper; green; white; sparkling; stern

3 him; It; his; his

blue pen:

1 diary; shock; room; boots; hook; door; pyjamas; pillow; books; pictures; place; wallpaper; eyes; words; dismissal

2 quite; slightly; breathlessly

3 down; around; from; behind; from under; in

verbs: put; looked; feeling; dazed; was; see; hanging; protruding; chattering; watching; intoned

connectives: and; as

7 Subjects and objects

(practice box, page 64)

a) the bird (s); hopped (v); the branches (o)
a) It hopped among them.
b) Susie and I (s); collected (v); conkers (o)
b) We collected them.
c) The hockey players (s); won (v); the competition (o)
c) They won it.

8 Gender and diminutives

(practice box, page 65)

Masculine	Feminine	Diminutive
drake	duck	duckling
fox	vixen	cub
waiter	waitress	
bull	cow	calf/bullock
uncle	aunt	
host	hostess	
bridegroom/groom	bride	
pig	sow	piglet
bachelor	spinster/bachelorette	

9 Synonyms and antonyms

(practice box, page 67)

	Synonym	Antonym
timid	shy	confident/bold
sorry	apologetic	unapologetic
cross	angry	good-tempered/cheerful
white		black
cautious	careful	reckless/rash
danger	peril/risk	safety/security
smooth	even/sleek	uneven/rough
courage	bravery/fearlessness	cowardice
single	one/unmarried	plural/married
good	fine/nice	bad/unpleasant

10 Abbreviations and acronyms

(practice box, page 68)

Abbreviations:
HQ = headquarters
GMT = Greenwich Mean Time
bus = omnibus
RSPCA = Royal Society for the Prevention of Cruelty to Animals
PTO = please turn over

Acronyms:
ASBO = Antisocial Behaviour Order
Ofcom = Office of Communications
ASH = Action on Smoking and Health
INSET = in-service education and training

11 Compound words

(practice box, page 69)

Examples are: overcoat; overarm; football; snowball; waistcoat; undercoat; waistline; underarm

12 Direct and reported speech

(practice box, page 70)

1. Dan told his mother that he would like a party for his birthday.
2. Mr Slater remarked that it felt like winter today.
3. The old man invited Charlie inside to have a cup of tea with them.

1. "Your behaviour is improving, children," said the headmistress.
2. "I'm feeling tired," complained my father.
3. "Have you remembered the note, Lisa?" asked her mother.

14 Practise the skills!

Punctuation test (Jules Verne extract, page 73)

How can I describe a vision of those rocks and those trees standing upright in those waters, their bases dark and sinister, their tops tinted by shades of red, intensified by the pure reflection of the water? We were scaling rocks that crumbled and let loose stones that crashed down behind us with the muffled rumble of an avalanche. To the right and the left were caves and grottos, hollowed out in the rocks, gloomy and impenetrable to the eyes. Elsewhere there were vast clearings, which seemed to have been created by human hands, and I wondered whether I might not suddenly come face-to-face with some inhabitant of these waters.

Paragraph exercise (Lewis Carroll extract, page 74)

"Have some wine," the March Hare said in an encouraging tone./ Alice looked all round the table, but there was nothing on it but tea. "I don't see any wine," she remarked./ "There isn't any," said the March Hare./ "Then it wasn't very civil of you to offer it," said Alice angrily./ "It wasn't very civil of you to sit down without being invited," said the March Hare./ "I didn't know it was your table," said Alice; "it's laid for a great many more than three."/ "Your hair wants cutting," said the Hatter. He had been looking at Alice for some time with great curiosity, and this was his first speech./ "You should learn not to make personal remarks," Alice said with some severity. "It's very rude."

E: Spelling

 Improve your spelling

(practice box, page 77)

Last year at **Christmas** our **family** had a **special** party with **thirty people**. My **aunt** and **uncle** came with their two **young children** and our **neighbours** from **across** the road **brought** their sons aged **thirteen** and **fourteen**. My **brother's friend** and his **mother walked** over from **around** the corner and **many other friends** and **family** were there.

We had drinks **between half** past ten and noon **followed** by **delicious** food. **During** lunch we **suddenly heard** a **great** bang **above** the kitchen and **something** crashed **through** the window.

We **thought possibly** the chimney had collapsed, but **gradually** realised the boys had **tried** out a new football which had **first** bounced off the kitchen roof and then broken the window!

The boys **immediately disappeared** before my **father told** them off and he **used** cardboard to mend the window. The **whole** party **could** have been spoilt **because** of this but one of our **friends** said at **first** he **thought** it was **Father Christmas** coming to join us, which made everyone **laugh**.

② *Learn awkward spellings*

Homophones

(practice box, page 78)

their; way; through; beech; wood; which; led; to; main; beach; knew; allowed; to; route; passed; course; where; their; practice; principal; beech; caught; their; hair; so; whole; hour; saw; coarse; waist.

Silent letters and unstressed vowels

(practice box, page 87)

bound**a**ry	bus**i**ness	conf**e**rence	dang**e**rous	def**i**nitely
diction**a**ry	diff**e**rent	eas**i**ly	extr**a**ordin**a**ry	event**ua**lly
fav**ou**rite	gen**e**rous	glam**o**rous	heav**e**n	hist**o**ry
hum**o**rous	int**e**resting	jewell**e**ry	nat**u**rally	**o**ccasion**a**lly

Adding suffixes

(practice box, page 90)

Examples are:

taking					
meaner	meanest	meaning	meaningful	meaningfully	meaningless
believable	believed	believer	believing		
noisier	noisiest	noisily			
arguable	argued	arguing	arguably	argument	
imaginable	imagined	imagining			
forced	forcer	forceful	forcing	forcefully	
worried	worrier	worrying	worryingly		
emptied	emptier	emptying			
related	relating	relation			

'-shun' suffixes

(practice box, page 91)

-tion:	competition	devotion	translation	explanation	direction	fiction	demonstration
-ssion:	possession	profession					
-cian:	optician	musician	electrician	politician			
-sion:	extension	collision	television				

Answers for pull-out test

1 E; **2** D; **3** D; **4** D; **5** D; **6** B; **7** A; **8** D; **9** E; **10** D; **11** C; **12** C; **13** B; **14** D; **15** D; **16** B; **17** E; **18** A; **19** B; **20** D; **21** C; **22** A; **23** C; **24** B; **25** D; **26** C; **27** X; **28** D; **29** A; **30** D; **31** B; **32** C; **33** D; **34** D; **35** C; **36** C; **37** A; **38** A; **39** B; **40** A; **41** X; **42** A; **43** B; **44** D; **45** B; **46** C; **47** D; **48** A; **49** B; **50** C